Systematic Theology Guide and Workbook for Teens

The Complete Bible Study to Understand Christian Doctrine and Live Out Your Faith with Confidence

TABLE OF CONTENTS

PART 2: SYSTEMATIC THEOLOGY WORKBOOK FOR TEENS

PART 1: SYSTEMATIC THEOLOGY FOR TEENS

A Clear Guide to What Christians Believe and Why It Matters

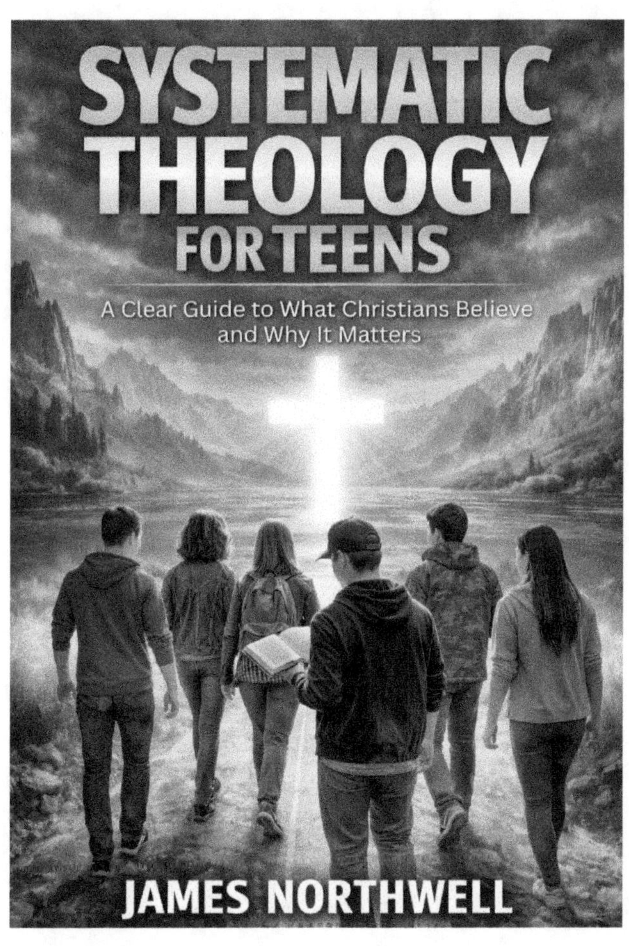

INTRODUCTION

WHY WHAT YOU BELIEVE CHANGES EVERYTHING

You make hundreds of choices every single day. You decide what to wear when you get up. You choose which friends to sit with at lunch. You pick which videos to watch or which games to play. Most of these choices feel small. They do not seem to change your life much. But under these small choices are much bigger ones.

You have views about who you are. You have ideas about right and wrong. You have thoughts about where the world came from and where it is going. These big ideas are like the OS on your phone. You might not see the code, but it runs every app you use. If the code is broken, the phone does not work right.

This book is about that "code." We are going to look at what Christians believe and why those beliefs matter. This is not just for people who want to be pastors. This is for you.

The name of this book is a bit of a mouthful. Let's break it down into simple terms.

Theology comes from two Greek words. *Theos* means "God" and *logos* means "word" or "study." So, theology is simply the study of God. It is the effort to know who God is and what He has done. If you have ever thought about God or asked a question about Him, you were doing theology.

Systematic means organized. Think about a library. If all the books were thrown in a giant pile in the middle of the floor, you would never find what you need. A library is helpful because it is organized. History is in one spot. Science is in another.

Systematic Theology is just an organized way of looking at the Bible. Instead of reading from page one to the end, we pick a topic. We look at everything the Bible says about that topic from start to finish. We put those truths together so we can see the whole picture clearly.

Why Does This Matter for You?

Some people think that "doctrine" or "theology" is boring. They think it is just for old books and dusty classrooms. They might say, "I just want to love Jesus. I don't need all that technical stuff."

But you cannot love someone you do not know. If you say you love your best friend but you think they are a 50-year-old man from Alaska when they are actually a 15-year-old girl from your town, you don't really love *them*. You love a version of them you made up.

Knowing the truth about God is the only way to love the real God. Here are three reasons why this study is vital:

- **It protects you from lies.** Plenty of people will tell you who God is. Some say He is a mean judge. Others say He is a cosmic Santa Claus who just wants you to be happy. Theology helps you compare those ideas to the Bible.

- **It gives you a solid foundation.** Life can get messy. Friends walk away. Grades drop. People get sick. If your faith is based only on a "feeling," it will shake when things go wrong. Knowing the character of God gives you a rock to stand on.

- **It leads to right living.** What you think about God changes how you treat people. It changes how you use your money and your time. Clear thinking leads to a life that honors Him.

> **"Do not conform to the pattern of this world, but be transformed by the renewing of your mind. Then you will be able to test and approve what God's will is—his good, pleasing and perfect will." - *Romans 12:2***

A God-Centered Approach

Many books for teens focus on "you." They talk about your dreams, your problems, and your potential. While those things matter, they are not the main point of the Bible.

The Bible is a book about God.

In this book, we will start with God. We will look at His nature, His plan, and His work. When you see how big and good God is, your own life starts to make sense. You find your value because He made you. You find your purpose because He called you. You find your hope because He saved you.

We will use the Bible as our primary tool. We believe that God has spoken clearly in His Word. We do not have to guess what He is like. He told us.

What to Expect

We have organized this guide into sections. Each part builds on the one before it. We will start with the Bible itself. Then we will look at God the Father, the problem of sin, and the work of Jesus. We will finish by looking at the church and what happens at the end of time.

As you read, you might find some ideas that are new to you. You might find things that are hard to grasp at first. That is okay. God is infinite. We are not. We should expect to find things about Him that are bigger than our own brains.

This is not a book you have to rush through. Take your time. Think about the verses. Ask God to help you see the truth. The goal is not just to finish the book. The goal is to know the Creator of the universe.

To get the most value out of these pages, try the following:

1. **Read with a Bible nearby.** Do not just take my word for it. Look up the verses yourself.

2. **Ask questions.** If something is confusing, talk to a parent, a youth leader, or a pastor.

3. **Apply it.** Every chapter ends with a section on why the topic matters. Do not skip this. Theology is meant to be lived, not just filed away.

Knowledge of God is the greatest treasure you can have. It is better than a high GPA, a big bank account, or a lot of followers. When you know who God is, you know the truth that sets you free.

Let's begin.

SECTION ONE
THE FOUNDATION

CHAPTER 1

THE BOOK GOD WROTE (THE BIBLE)

Imagine you are walking through a thick forest. The trees are tall, and the brush is so dense you can barely see your own feet. You have no map and no cell service. You feel lost. Suddenly, you look down and see a clear, well-lit path. Even better, there is a guide waiting for you who knows every inch of the woods. He has a letter for you that explains exactly how to get home.

Life often feels like that forest. You face big questions about your future, your identity, and what is true. You do not have to guess the answers. God did not leave us to wander in the dark. He spoke. He gave us a book to show us who He is and how we should live. We call this book the Bible.

God Is Not Silent

The most important thing to know about God is that He wants to be known. He is not a distant force hiding behind the clouds. He is a person who communicates. In theology, we use the word **revelation** to describe God showing Himself to us.

Think about meeting a new person. You can look at their clothes or their hair to learn a little bit about them. But you will never really know their heart until they speak to you. God has "spoken" to us in two main ways.

1. The World Around Us (General Revelation)

God speaks through what He made. When you look at a sunset or the vastness of the ocean, you see His power. When you look at the tiny details of a leaf or the human eye, you see His wisdom. The stars tell us that God is great.

This is called "general" because it is available to everyone, everywhere. You do not need a Bible to see that a Creator exists. Psalm 19:1 says, "The heavens declare the glory of God, and the sky above proclaims his handiwork." Nature is like a giant billboard pointing to God.

2. The Word of God (Special Revelation)

Nature tells us God is powerful, but it does not tell us His name. It does not tell us how He feels about sin or how we can be saved. For that, we need "special" revelation. This is where God uses words.

God spoke through prophets. He spoke through His Son, Jesus. And He gave us the Bible so we would have a permanent record of His truth. The Bible is God's specific message to us.

Where Did the Bible Come From?

If you look at the Bible, you will see it is a big book made of 66 smaller books. It was written by about 40 different men over a span of 1,500 years. These men were kings, farmers, doctors, and fishermen. They wrote in different languages and lived in different countries.

Yet, when you read the Bible, it tells one single, perfect story. It does not contradict itself. How is that possible?

The answer is **inspiration**.

> **"All Scripture is God-breathed and is useful for teaching, rebuking, correcting and training in righteousness," -**
> *2 Timothy 3:16*

When the Bible says Scripture is "breathed out" by God, it means He is the ultimate source. The human authors were not like robots. God did not put them in a trance and take over their hands. They used their own styles and personalities. But the Holy Spirit guided them so perfectly that every word they wrote was exactly what God wanted to say.

Because God is the real author, the Bible is different from any other book on your shelf. It is not just a collection of human ideas. It is the Word of the Living God.

Since God is perfect and cannot lie, His Word is perfect too. We use the word **inerrancy** to describe this. It means the Bible, in its original form, does not have any errors. It is completely true in everything it teaches.

Some people might tell you the Bible is just full of myths. But the more we learn about history and archaeology, the more the Bible is proven right. It describes real people, real places, and real events.

Even more importantly, the Bible is **sufficient**. This means it gives us everything we need to know for a life of faith. We do not need new messages or "secret" codes. If we want to know what God thinks about a topic, we look at the Bible. It is the final authority for what we believe and how we act.

The Purpose of the Bible

God did not give us the Bible just so we could win a trivia game. He gave it to us to change us.

- **It shows us our need.** The Bible is like a mirror. It shows us our sin and our need for a Savior.

- **It points to Jesus.** From the first page to the last, the Bible is about God's plan to rescue us through Christ.

- **It guides our steps.** Psalm 119:105 says, "Your word is a lamp to my feet and a light to my path." It helps us make wise choices in a confusing world.

- **It feeds our souls.** Just as your body needs food to grow, your spirit needs the Word of God to stay healthy.

How to Approach the Bible

Since the Bible is God's Word, we should treat it with respect. It is not a book you read once and put away. It is a book you live in.

Try to read it every day. You do not have to read five chapters at a time. Even a few verses can give you something to think about all day. When you read, ask God to help you see what He wants to show you.

Do not be discouraged if some parts are hard to understand. Some parts of the Bible are like deep water. You can keep swimming in them for your whole life and still find new things. The main message, however, is clear: God loves us, we are sinners, and Jesus is the way home.

Why This Matters to You

What you think about the Bible changes how you hear God. If the Bible is just a human book, you can pick and choose which parts to follow. You can ignore the parts that are hard or the parts you do not like.

But if the Bible is the Word of God, it has authority over your life. When you read it, you are listening to your Creator. You can trust it when you are sad. You can lean on it when you are afraid. You can build your whole life on its promises, and you will never be let down.

Knowing that God wrote a book for you is a beautiful thing. It means you are never truly lost. You have a guide. You have a map. You have the truth.

Reflect and Talk

1. If the Bible is "breathed out" by God, how should that change the way you feel when you open it?

2. Have you ever felt like nature was "speaking" to you about God? What did it say?

3. What is one area of your life where you need the Bible to be a "lamp to your feet" right now?

CHAPTER 2

IS THE BIBLE TRUE?

It is one thing to say the Bible is God's Word. It is another thing to believe it when your friends, your teachers, or people on the internet say it is a book of fairytales. Maybe you have sat in your room and wondered, *How do I really know this is true?* Asking questions is not a sign of weak faith. God is not afraid of your questions. He made your mind, and He wants you to use it. We do not have to check our brains at the door to believe the Bible. In fact, the more we look at the evidence, the more we see that the Bible is the most reliable book in history.

The Amazing Puzzle

In the last chapter, we mentioned that the Bible has about 40 authors. Think about that for a second. Imagine you gathered 40 people from different countries. Some are from the 1800s, some from the 1900s, and some from today. They speak different languages. They have different jobs.

Now, ask each of them to write one chapter of a book about the meaning of life. If you put those chapters together, what would you get? You would get a mess. The writers would disagree on almost everything.

But the Bible is different. Even though it was written over 1,500 years by men who often never met, it tells one unified story. It has one clear theme: God's plan to rescue people through Jesus. Every "piece" of the puzzle fits perfectly. This unity is a miracle. It shows that one Mind was behind the whole thing.

Promises Kept

One of the best ways to know if someone is telling the truth is to see if they keep their promises. The Bible is full of **prophecies**. These are moments where God told people what would happen hundreds of years before it took place.

If a psychic predicts that it will rain tomorrow, that is a guess. If a prophet predicts that a specific person will be born in a specific town and die in a specific way 700 years later, that is God.

The Old Testament contains hundreds of these details about Jesus.

- **His Birth:** Micah 5:2 said He would be born in Bethlehem.
- **His Rejection:** Isaiah 53 said His own people would turn against Him.
- **His Death:** Psalm 22 described His hands and feet being pierced long before the Romans even invented crucifixion.

The odds of one man fulfilling just eight of these prophecies by chance are nearly impossible. Jesus fulfilled all of them. God used these "receipts" to prove that His Word is true.

The Dirt Does Not Lie

Some people think the Bible is just a book of myths like the stories of Greek gods. But myths usually happen in "a land far, far away" at an unknown time. The Bible is different. It names real cities, real kings, and real dates.

For a long time, some critics said the Bible was wrong about certain groups of people, like the Hittites. They claimed the Hittites never existed. Then, in the early 1900s, archaeologists dug into the dirt and found the ruins of the Hittite capital. They found their records and their art. The Bible was right all along.

We also have the **Dead Sea Scrolls**. These are ancient copies of the Bible found in caves in 1947. They are over 2,000 years old. When scholars compared these ancient scrolls to the Bibles we have today, they were almost identical. This proves that the Bible has not been changed or corrupted over time. God has preserved His message.

The Witness of Jesus

If you want to know if the Bible is true, look at what Jesus thought. Jesus is the center of our faith. He rose from the dead, which proves He is who He said He is.

When Jesus was on earth, He quoted the Bible constantly. He called it "the commandment of God." He treated the stories of Adam and Eve,

Noah, and Jonah as real history. He never corrected the Bible. Instead, He used it to defeat the devil and to teach His followers.

If we trust Jesus with our lives, we should trust the book He loved. He believed every word was true.

The Power to Change Lives

There is one more kind of evidence that is very personal. It is the evidence of a changed life.

No other book has the power that the Bible has. Millions of people throughout history have been changed by its words.

- It has turned angry people into kind leaders.
- It has given hope to people who wanted to give up.
- It has given peace to people in the middle of wars.

When you read the Bible, it does not just give you information. It speaks to your heart. It tells you the truth about yourself, even the parts you try to hide. Then it shows you the grace of God that covers those parts. You can know the Bible is true because you can see it working in the world and in your own soul.

> **"The law of the Lord is perfect, refreshing the soul. The statutes of the Lord are trustworthy, making wise the simple." - *Psalm 19:7***

Faith and Facts

Does this mean we have every single answer? No. There are still things in history we are learning. There are still passages that are hard to understand.

But faith is not "blind." Blind faith is believing in something when there is no reason to. Biblical faith is trusting in God because He has shown Himself to be trustworthy. We have enough evidence to know that the Bible is a solid foundation. You can build your life on it without being afraid that it will crack.

If the Bible is just a book of opinions, you do not have to listen to it. You can do whatever feels right in the moment. You can follow the crowd or do what is popular on social media.

But if the Bible is true, you have an anchor. When the world feels chaotic and everyone is shouting different "truths," you have the real Truth.

- You don't have to wonder if you matter; God says you do.
- You don't have to wonder if there is hope for the world; God says there is.
- You don't have to guess how to live a good life; God has given you the map.

Believing the Bible is true gives you a confidence that nothing else can. It means that when you open your Bible, you aren't just reading ancient history. You are hearing from the Creator who knows you by name.

Reflect and Talk

1. Which piece of evidence, unity, prophecy, archaeology, or changed lives, is most helpful to you when you have doubts?
2. Why is it important that the Bible mentions real places and real people instead of being a "long time ago in a galaxy far away"?
3. If you really believed the Bible was 100% true, how would that change the way you read it tomorrow morning?

SECTION TWO

THE CREATOR

CHAPTER 3

WHO IS GOD?

If you want to know what someone is like, you look at their actions. You listen to their words. You see how they treat others. Learning about God is no different. But there is one big problem. God is much bigger than we are. Trying to understand God is a bit like an ant trying to understand how the internet works. The ant can see the router and feel the warmth of the wires. But it cannot grasp the code or the vast network behind it.

Thankfully, God has not left us guessing. He has told us about His character. In this chapter, we will look at who God is. We will see that He is not just a "force" or a "vibe." He is a living Person with specific traits. These traits tell us that He is worthy of our trust and our worship.

God Is Spirit and He Is One

Before we look at what God *does*, we have to look at what God *is*. The Bible tells us: "God is spirit, and his worshipers must worship in the Spirit and in truth." (John 4:24). This means He does not have a physical body like we do. He is not made of skin, bones, or atoms. Because He is spirit, He is not limited by space or time. He does not get tired. He does not need to sleep or eat.

The Bible also teaches that there is only one God. This is called **monotheism.** In the ancient world, people worshipped hundreds of different gods. They had a god for the sun, a god for the rain, and a god for the crops. But the Bible is clear: "The Lord our God, the Lord is one" (Deuteronomy 6:4). Everything in the universe was made by this one Creator.

God Has a Name

God is not just a title. He has a personal name. In the Old Testament, God revealed His name to Moses as **Yahweh.** In English, we often translate this as "The LORD" (in all capital letters).

The name Yahweh means "I Am Who I Am." It tells us that God is self-existent. He does not need anything from us. He did not need to be created. He has always been there, and He will always be there. He is the source of all life. When we call on God, we are calling on a Person who is completely independent and eternal.

Attributes You Cannot Share

Theologians often split God's traits into two groups. The first group includes things that are true *only* of God. No human can ever have these traits. These help us see how great He is.

1. God Knows Everything (Omniscience)

God has never learned a new fact. He has never had an "aha!" moment. He knows everything that has happened, everything that is happening, and everything that will ever happen. He even knows your secret thoughts and your future choices. Psalm 139:4 says, "Even before a word is on my tongue, behold, O Lord, you know it altogether."

2. God Is Everywhere (Omnipresence)

There is no place you can go where God is not present. He is in the highest heaven and the deepest ocean. He is with you in your bedroom and He is with a believer on the other side of the planet at the exact same time. This does not mean God *is* the trees or the rocks. It means He is present everywhere in His creation.

3. God Is All-Powerful (Omnipotence)

God can do anything that is consistent with His character. He created the entire universe out of nothing just by speaking. He sustains the stars and keeps the planets in orbit. There is no problem in your life that is too big for Him. Nothing is too hard for the Lord.

4. God Never Changes (Immutability)

The world changes every day. Fashion changes. Technology changes. Even your best friends might change. But God never changes. His character, His promises, and His truth are the same today as they were thousands of years ago. You can count on Him because: "Every good and perfect gift is from above, coming down from the Father of the heavenly lights, who does not change like shifting shadows." (James 1:17).

The second group of traits includes things that God has, but that we can also have (in a much smaller way). God made us in His image, so we can reflect these parts of His character.

- **God is Holy:** To be "holy" means to be set apart or "cut off" from everything else. God is perfectly pure. There is no sin in Him. He is the standard for what is good and right.

- **God is Just:** God always does what is right. He is a perfect Judge. He cannot ignore sin, and He will make sure that justice is done in the end. He is fair in all His ways.

- **God is Love:** This is not just something God does; it is who He is. His love is not a "crush" or a feeling that comes and goes. It is a steady, sacrificial commitment to the good of others. He showed this most clearly by sending Jesus to die for us.

- **God is Truth:** God is the source of all truth. He cannot lie. Everything He says is a perfect match for reality. You can trust His Word because it is impossible for Him to be wrong.

"Each of the four living creatures had six wings and was covered with eyes all around, even under its wings. Day and night they never stop saying: "'Holy, holy, holy is the Lord God Almighty, who was, and is, and is to come.'" -
Revelation 4:8

Why This Matters to You

Knowing who God is changes how you see your daily life. If God were just a powerful force, you might be afraid of Him. If He were just a loving friend, you might not respect Him. But because He is both great and good, you can rest.

When you feel lonely, remember His omnipresence. You are never truly alone. The Creator of the stars is right there in the room with you.

When you feel confused, remember His omniscience. You do not have to have all the answers for your life. God already knows the path ahead. He is not surprised by the things that surprise you.

When you feel guilty, remember His holiness and His love. His holiness shows you that your sin is serious. But His love tells you that He has provided a way for you to be forgiven and brought back to Him.

When the world feels out of control, remember His omnipotence and immutability. Politicians may fail and the economy may crash. But the God who runs the universe is still on His throne. He is not shaking or worried. He is the same yesterday, today, and forever.

God Is Greater Than Our Ideas

As you learn these things, you might feel like your head is spinning. That is a good sign! If we could fit God inside our small minds, He wouldn't be much of a God. He is supposed to be bigger than us.

We study these truths so we can worship Him for who He really is. We don't want to worship a "god" we made up in our own heads. We want to know the real God—the one who is all-knowing, all-present, all-powerful, and perfectly loving.

Reflect and Talk

1. Which of the "Omni" words (Omniscience, Omnipresent, Omnipotent) gives you the most comfort right now? Why?

2. Why is it important that God never changes? How would your life feel if God changed His mind about His promises?

3. Since God is holy and pure, how should that change the way we think about the "little" sins we often ignore?

CHAPTER 4

THREE PERSONS, ONE GOD (THE TRINITY)

Most math is easy. One plus one plus one equals three. But when we look at who God is, we find a different kind of math. One plus one plus one equals one. This is the doctrine of the Trinity.

The word "Trinity" is not actually in the Bible. Christians created the word to describe a truth that appears on almost every page of Scripture. It is the belief that there is one God who exists eternally in three Persons: the Father, the Son, and the Holy Spirit.

If this feels hard to grasp, you are in good company. We are trying to describe a Creator who is far beyond our logic. But even if we cannot fully explain it, we can look at what God has told us.

The Basic Idea

To get the best start, we need to distinguish between a "Being" and a "Person."

- **Being** is the "What."
- **Person** is the "Who."

You are one being and one person. God is different. He is one Being (the only true God) but He is three Persons. These three Persons are not three separate gods. They are not three different "modes" of God. They are distinct, yet they are the same God. They have always existed together in perfect love.

Where Is This in the Bible?

The Bible makes two things very clear from the start. First, there is only one God. Second, the Father is God, Jesus is God, and the Holy Spirit is God.

1. The Old Testament Hints

Even in the first chapter of the Bible, we see hints. In Genesis 1:26, God says, "Let **us** make man in **our** image." Who is the "us"? God is talking within Himself. We see the Spirit of God hovering over the waters in the beginning. We see a God who is one, but also a plural "us."

2. The Baptism of Jesus

One of the clearest pictures of the Trinity happens when Jesus gets baptized.

- **The Son** (Jesus) is standing in the water.
- **The Holy Spirit** comes down like a dove.
- **The Father** speaks from heaven, saying, "This is my beloved Son."

All three Persons are present and active at the same time. They are not one person changing costumes. They are three distinct Persons acting together.

3. The Great Commission

Before Jesus went back to heaven, He told His followers to baptize new believers "in the **name** of the Father and of the Son and of the Holy Spirit" (Matthew 28:19). Notice He said "name" (singular), not "names" (plural). One name, three Persons.

Avoid the Common Mistakes

People often try to use analogies to explain the Trinity. While they try to help, most of them actually teach something wrong about God.

- **The Water Analogy:** Some say God is like water. It can be ice, liquid, or steam. This is an error called "Modalism." Water cannot be all three at the same time in the same way. But the Father, Son, and Spirit are always distinct.

- **The Egg Analogy:** Some say God is like an egg. It has a shell, a white, and a yolk. This is an error called "Partialism." It suggests that the Father is only one-third of God. In reality, each Person is fully God.

- **The Three-Leaf Clover:** This also suggests that each Person is just a piece of God.

It is better to admit that God is a mystery than to use a bad example that makes Him smaller than He is. God is unique. Nothing else in the universe is like Him.

While the Father, Son, and Spirit are all equal in power and glory, they often take on different roles in our lives.

- **The Father** is the Planner. He is the one who chose to create the world. He sent the Son to save us. He is the source of all things.

- **The Son** (Jesus) is the Redeemer. He is the one who became a human. He lived the perfect life we could not live. He died on the cross and rose again. He is the one who makes us right with God.

- **The Holy Spirit** is the Helper. He is the one who lives inside believers. He gives us the strength to follow Jesus. He helps us pray and helps us grasp the truth of the Bible.

Think of a song with three-part harmony. It is one song, but each voice has a different part. When they sing together, it creates a beauty that one voice could not make alone.

"May the grace of the Lord Jesus Christ, and the love of God, and the fellowship of the Holy Spirit be with you all." -
2 Corinthians 13:14

Why This Matters to You

You might ask, "Does it really matter if God is three or one?" It matters for one very big reason: **Love.**

If God were only one Person, He could not have been "love" before He created the world. Who would He have loved? He would have been lonely. He would have needed to create us just to have someone to love.

But because God is a Trinity, He has always been in a relationship. The Father has loved the Son and the Spirit for all eternity. God does not *need* us. He is already perfectly happy and full of love within Himself.

This means He created you not because He was lonely, but because He wanted to share His love with you.

- **You are invited into a family.** When you follow Jesus, you are brought into the relationship that the Father, Son, and Spirit have enjoyed forever.

- **You have a model for community.** We were made to live with others because we were made by a God who lives in community.

- **Your salvation is secure.** Your rescue was planned by the Father, finished by the Son, and is kept safe by the Spirit.

Knowing the Trinity helps you see that God is not a cold, lonely force. He is a living, loving community. When you pray, you speak to the Father, through the Son, by the help of the Spirit. You are never alone.

Reflect and Talk

1. Why is it actually a good thing that we cannot fully explain the Trinity with our own logic?

2. How does the idea of God being a "community of Persons" change the way you think about your own friendships?

3. Look at the baptism of Jesus in Matthew 3:13–17. How do you see the three Persons working together in that moment?

CHAPTER 5

CREATOR OF ALL THINGS

Think about the last thing you made. Maybe it was a sketch in a notebook, a *level* in a video game, or a batch of cookies. To make those things, you needed materials. You needed paper and a pencil. You needed code and a computer. You needed flour, sugar, and an oven. Humans are great at "making" things, but we always start with something that already exists.

God is different. When God created the universe, He did not have a toolbox. He did not have a pile of star-dust or a set of blueprints. He started with nothing. In this chapter, we look at how God brought everything into existence and why that changes how you look at the world around you.

Everything from Nothing

The very first verse of the Bible says: *"In the beginning God created the heavens and the earth"* (Genesis 1:1). This tells us that before the universe began, there was only God. There was no space, no time, and no matter.

Theologians use a Latin phrase for this: *creatio ex nihilo*. It simply means "creation out of nothing."

How did He do it? He spoke. He did not have to sweat or struggle. He said, "Let there be light," and light existed. This shows us the sheer power of God's word. When God speaks, reality changes. The stars, the planets, the deep oceans, and the microscopic cells in your body all exist because God willed them to be. They are not accidents. They are the result of a deliberate, intelligent choice by a powerful Creator.

The Universe Is a Mirror

God did not just make a "blank" universe. He filled it with variety, color, and order. Every part of creation tells us something about the Person who made it.

- **His Power:** Think about the sun. It is a massive ball of fire 93 million miles away. It is so powerful that it keeps our whole solar system in place. Yet, it is just one of billions of stars. The God who made the sun is much more powerful than the sun itself.

- **His Wisdom:** Look at the way an ecosystem works. Plants make oxygen. Animals breathe it. The water cycle moves rain from the sea to the fields. Everything is timed perfectly. This shows that God is a Master Designer.

- **His Beauty:** Why are there so many shades of blue in the ocean? Why do sunsets turn purple and orange? God did not have to make the world beautiful for it to work, but He did. This tells us He is a God who loves beauty.

When you look at nature, you are looking at God's artwork. It is meant to point you back to Him.

It Was "Very Good"

In Genesis 1, God stops after each day of work to look at what He made. He says, "It is good." At the very end, He looks at everything together and says it is "very good."

This is important because some people think the physical world is bad or "lesser" than spiritual things. They think that only "church stuff" matters to God. But that is not true. God made the physical world. He made your body. He made the food you eat and the air you breathe.

Because God made these things, they have value.

- Science is a way of studying God's handiwork.
- Art is a way of reflecting God's creativity.
- Athletics is a way of using the bodies God designed.

The world is broken now because of sin (which we will talk about later), but the "stuff" of the world is still fundamentally good because it belongs to God.

Creator vs. Creation

It is easy to get confused about the relationship between God and His world. There are two main mistakes people make:

1. **Thinking God is the world (Pantheism):** Some people believe that God *is* the trees, the stars, and the people. They think the universe is just part of God. The Bible says no. God is distinct from what He made. A painter is not the same thing as the painting.

2. **Thinking God is far away (Deism):** Some believe God made the world like a clock, wound it up, and then walked away. They think He doesn't care what happens now. The Bible says no to this, too. God is "sustaining all things by his powerful word" (Hebrews 1:3). If God stopped thinking about the universe for one second, it would cease to exist.

God is above the world (transcendent) but He is also very close to the world (immanent). He is the King of the universe, but He also counts the hairs on your head.

> **"For in him all things were created: things in heaven and on earth, visible and invisible, whether thrones or powers or rulers or authorities; all things have been created through him and for him."** - *Colossians 1:16*

The "Why" Behind the "What"

Why did God bother to make all of this? He didn't need us. As we learned in the chapter on the Trinity, God was already perfectly happy and loved within Himself.

God created the world for His **glory**.

Think of a "glory" like a great light or a reputation. God wanted to put His character on display. He wanted to share His goodness and His joy with others. The universe is like a giant stage where God's story is being told. Every mountain, every whale, and every human being exists to show how great God is.

When we live for our own glory, we feel empty. We were not made to be the center of the story. When we live for God's glory, we find our true purpose. We are like small mirrors reflecting a massive Sun.

Understanding God as Creator changes your perspective on three things:

1. Your Value You are not a cosmic accident. You are not just a collection of chemicals that happened to stick together. You were planned. God thought of you before the world began. He designed your DNA. He gave you your specific talents and your personality. You have value because the Creator of the universe made you on purpose.

2. Your Stewardship If God made the world, it belongs to Him. We are just "renters" or "managers." This means we should take care of the earth. We should treat animals with kindness. We should use the environment wisely. We don't protect nature because we worship nature; we protect nature because we love the One who made it.

3. Your Worship When you see something amazing, like a huge mountain range or a photo from a space telescope, your first instinct is to say, "Wow!" That "wow" is actually the beginning of worship. Don't stop at being amazed by the thing. Be amazed by the God who made the thing. The universe is a finger pointing toward God. Don't just stare at the finger; look where it is pointing.

Reflect and Talk

1. If God made everything "out of nothing," what does that tell you about His ability to handle the problems in your life?

2. What is your favorite part of creation (a specific animal, a type of weather, a place)? What does that specific thing tell you about God's personality?

3. How does knowing you were "made on purpose" change how you feel about yourself on a bad day?

SECTION THREE

THE PROBLEM

CHAPTER 6

BUILT IN HIS IMAGE

If you go to a zoo, you might spend time watching the chimpanzees. They are smart. They use tools to get food. They play with each other. They even seem to have feelings. You might look at them and think, *They are almost like us.* But there is a massive gap between the smartest animal and the simplest human being.

You can write a poem. You can pray. You can feel guilt when you do something wrong. You can plan for a future that is decades away. Where do these abilities come from? The Bible gives a specific answer. It says that humans are the crown of creation. We are the only part of the world that God made "in His image."

What Is the Image of God?

In Genesis 1:26, God says, "Then God said, "Let us make mankind in our image, in our likeness, so that they may rule over the fish in the sea and the birds in the sky, over the livestock and all the wild animals, and over all the creatures that move along the ground." Theologians call this the **Imago Dei**.

This does not mean God has a physical body and we look like Him. As we learned, God is spirit. Being made in His image means we reflect His character. We are like small mirrors designed to show what God is like to the rest of the world.

There are four main ways we reflect the image of God:

1. We Can Think (Rationality)

God has a mind. He plans and designs. He gave us the ability to think, reason, and solve problems. We can use logic. We can learn languages and tell stories. No other creature on earth can study the stars or write a symphony. We have an intellect because God has an intellect.

2. We Can Choose (Morality)

Animals act on instinct. A lion does not feel "guilty" for hunting a zebra. It is just doing what lions do. But you have a conscience. You have a sense of right and wrong. You know that some things are fair and others are cruel. This moral sense comes from God, who is perfectly holy and just.

3. We Can Love (Relationships)

God is a Trinity. He has lived in a relationship of love forever. Because He made us in His image, we are social beings. We crave friendship. We want to be known and loved. We find our greatest joy when we are in a healthy relationship with God and with other people.

4. We Can Create (Creativity)

God is the Great Creator. He made the world out of nothing. We cannot make things out of nothing, but we love to take what is already here and turn it into something new. Whether you are coding a website, painting a picture, or building a shelf, you are using the creative spark God put inside you.

Our Job Description

God did not just make us to look like Him. He gave us a job to do: "God blessed them and said to them, "Be fruitful and increase in number; fill the earth and subdue it. Rule over the fish in the sea and the birds in the sky and over every living creature that moves on the ground." (Genesis 1:28).

This is not a license to be a bully or to ruin the planet. It means we are God's "vice-regents." Think of a king who goes on a trip and leaves his son in charge of the palace. The son does not own the palace, but he is responsible for making sure everything runs well.

We are called to manage the world on God's behalf. We are meant to bring order out of chaos. We are meant to help things grow and flourish. When we take care of the environment, help the poor, or invent things that make life better, we are doing the job God gave us.

This truth is the most important foundation for how we treat people. Why is it wrong to bully someone? Why is it wrong to ignore someone who is suffering? Why do we care about the elderly or people with disabilities?

In a world without God, people often decide value based on what you can *do*. If you are smart, rich, or athletic, you have value. If you are weak or "unproductive," you don't.

But the Bible says your value is not based on what you do. It is based on who you *are*. Every single human being, no matter their race, their age, or their health, is a bearer of the image of God.

- The person who disagrees with you is an image-bearer.
- The person on the other side of the world is an image-bearer.
- The person you find difficult to like is an image-bearer.

If you insult a person, you are insulting the God who made them. If you show kindness to a person, you are honoring the Image of God.

> **"With the tongue we praise our Lord and Father, and with it we curse human beings, who have been made in God's likeness. Out of the same mouth come praise and cursing. My brothers and sisters, this should not be." - *James 3:9-10***

A Broken Mirror

We have to be honest. While we are made in God's image, we don't always act like it. If you drop a mirror on the floor, it shatters. It is still a mirror. It still reflects light. But the reflection is now distorted and cracked.

That is what happened to us. Because of sin (which we will study in the next chapter), the image of God in us is broken. We still have the ability to think, love, and create, but we often use those gifts for the wrong reasons. We use our minds to lie. We use our creativity to hurt others.

The good news of the Bible is that God is in the business of fixing the mirror. When we follow Jesus, God begins to restore His image in us. He starts to make us look like Him again.

1. You Have Instant Value You live in a world that constantly tells you that you aren't enough. You aren't thin enough, smart enough, or popular enough. The doctrine of the *Imago Dei* shuts those lies down. You have dignity because God stamped His image on your soul. You don't have to earn your worth. You were born with it.

2. You Have a Purpose You are not here to just exist and then die. You are here to represent God. Every day is a chance to show the world what God is like through your words and your actions. You are an ambassador for the King of the universe.

3. You Have a Reason to Respect Others This changes how you walk down the hallways at school. It changes how you talk to your parents. Every person you see is a "masterpiece" of God's creation. Even the people who are hard to love deserve your respect because of whose image they carry.

Reflect and Talk

1. Which of the four ways we reflect God (thinking, choosing, loving, creating) do you feel is strongest in your life right now?

2. How would our schools or social media change if every teen treated others as "image-bearers" of God?

3. Knowing that you were made to "reflect" God, what is one thing about His character you want people to see when they look at your life?

CHAPTER 7

WHAT WENT WRONG?

If you spend five minutes watching the news or scrolling through social media, you see a clear pattern. The world is a mess. We see wars, poverty, and people treating each other with cruelty. Even in your own life, you feel it. You feel the sting of a friend's lie. You feel the sadness of losing a grandparent. You feel the frustration of your own mistakes.

In the last chapter, we saw that God made everything "very good." So, what happened? Why is the world so full of pain? The Bible does not shy away from this question. It tells us that a great disaster occurred early in human history. This disaster changed everything. We call it "The Fall."

The Choice in the Garden

God placed the first two humans, Adam and Eve, in a perfect garden. They had everything they needed. They had a perfect relationship with God and with each other. But God did not want them to be robots. Love is only real if it is a choice.

To give them a choice, God gave them one rule. They could eat from any tree in the garden except for one: the Tree of the Knowledge of Good and Evil. God warned them that if they ate from it, they would die.

Then came the serpent: "Now the serpent was more crafty than any of the wild animals the Lord God had made. He said to the woman, "Did God really say, 'You must not eat from any tree in the garden'?"(Genesis 3:1).

He convinced them that God was holding out on them. He told them that if they ate the fruit, they would be like God.

Adam and Eve chose to trust the serpent instead of their Creator. They took the fruit and ate. In that moment, the "very good" world was shattered.

We often think of sin as a list of "bad things" like lying or stealing. While those are sins, the root of sin is much deeper.

The word "sin" in the Bible often comes from an archery term that means **"to miss the mark."** Imagine an archer aiming at a bullseye. If the arrow lands anywhere else, he missed the mark. God is the bullseye. He is the standard of perfection. Anything we do, think, or say that falls short of His perfect character is sin.

At its heart, sin is **rebellion**. It is telling God, "I know better than You. I want to be the boss of my own life. I want to set my own rules." It is a rejection of God's authority and a lack of trust in His goodness.

When Adam and Eve sinned, the consequences were immediate. Sin acted like a spiritual earthquake that cracked the foundation of every relationship.

1. Our Relationship with God

Before the Fall, Adam and Eve talked with God face-to-face. After they sinned, they felt shame for the first time. They tried to hide from God among the trees. Sin creates a wall between us and a holy God. Because God is life, turning away from Him leads to death.

2. Our Relationship with Ourselves

Sin brought shame and fear. We no longer feel "at home" in our own skin. We struggle with guilt, anxiety, and a sense that something is "off" inside of us. We are no longer the perfect reflection of God we were meant to be.

3. Our Relationship with Others

As soon as God asked Adam what happened, Adam blamed Eve. Eve blamed the Serpent. The perfect harmony between humans was gone. Now, we have conflict, jealousy, and war. Every argument you have with your parents or friends is a result of the Fall.

4. Our Relationship with Nature

Even the earth itself changed. God told Adam that the ground would now produce thorns and thistles. Work would be hard. Bodies would get sick and eventually die. The natural world is now "groaning" for everything to be made right again.

Theologians use a heavy term to describe our current state: **Total Depravity**.

This does not mean that every person is as bad as they could possibly be. It does not mean you never do anything kind or helpful. It means that sin has touched every single part of who you are.

Think of a glass of water. If you put one drop of black ink into the glass, the ink spreads. It touches every molecule of the water. You can no longer say the water is pure.

In the same way, sin has affected our minds, our emotions, our bodies, and our wills. We are born with a "sin nature." This is why a toddler does not have to be taught how to throw a tantrum or hit a sibling. We are born with a heart that naturally wanders away from God.

"As it is written: "There is no one righteous, not even one; there is no one who understands; there is no one who seeks God. All have turned away, they have together become worthless; there is no one who does good, not even one."- *Romans 3:10–12*

The First Hint of Hope

If the story ended there, it would be the most depressing book ever written. But right in the middle of the mess, God gave a promise.

While God was explaining the consequences of sin to the serpent, He said something strange: "And I will put enmity between you and the woman, and between your offspring and hers; he will crush your head, and you will strike his heel." (Genesis 3:15).

This is the first "Gospel" message in the Bible. God promised that one day, a human descendant would come to crush the head of the Serpent. This Savior would be "bruised" in the process, but He would win the final victory. Even before Adam and Eve left the garden, God had a rescue plan in motion.

1. It Explains Reality Have you ever wondered why it is so hard to be "good"? Have you wondered why there is so much hate in the world? The doctrine of the Fall gives you the answer. You don't have to be confused by the darkness. You know why it is there.

2. It Keeps You Humble Knowing that you have a sin nature stops you from being "judgey" toward others. You realize that you have the same capacity for wrong as anyone else. You see that you cannot fix yourself. You are not just a "good person who makes mistakes." You are a person in need of a rescue.

3. It Points You to Your True Need If our main problem was a lack of information, we would just need better schools. If our main problem was poverty, we would just need more money. But if our main problem is sin, we need a Savior.

Understanding what went wrong is the only way to appreciate what God did to fix it. You have to know the bad news before the Good News makes any sense. You are a broken image-bearer, but you are still loved by the God who wants to put the pieces back together.

Reflect and Talk

1. When you look at the world today, where do you see the "thorns and thistles" of the Fall most clearly?

2. Why is it easier to blame someone else (like Adam did) than to admit our own part in a problem?

3. How does knowing that every person is "fallen" change the way you look at people who have hurt you?

SECTION FOUR
THE RESCUE

CHAPTER 8

WHO IS JESUS?

In the last chapter, we looked at the "Bad News." Humans broke the world through sin, and we cannot fix it ourselves. If the story ended there, it would be a tragedy. But the heart of the Bible is the "Good News" about a Person.

If you ask people on the street who Jesus is, you will get many answers. Some say He was a great moral teacher. Others say He was a social revolutionary or a prophet. But the Bible makes a claim that is much more shocking. It tells us that Jesus is the Son of God who became a man to save us. To understand theology, you must understand the person of Jesus Christ.

Fully God: The Word Was God

The Bible begins the story of Jesus long before He was born in a manger. The Apostle John tells us that "In the beginning was the Word, and the Word was with God, and the Word was God" (John 1:1). Jesus didn't start existing in Bethlehem. He has existed forever as the second Person of the Trinity.

There are three big reasons we know Jesus is fully God:

1. **He did what only God can do.** He calmed storms with a word, walked on water, and raised people from the dead. Most importantly, He forgave sins; something the religious leaders of His day rightly said only God has the authority to do.

2. **He claimed to be God.** Jesus said, "I and the Father are one" (John 10:30). He used the name "I AM" for Himself, which was the sacred name God gave to Moses.

3. **He accepted worship.** In the Bible, good men and angels always refuse worship. But Jesus allowed people to bow down and worship Him as Lord.

If Jesus is not God, He cannot save us. A mere man cannot pay for the sins of the whole world. Only the infinite God can pay an infinite debt.

Fully Man: The Word Became Flesh

The most amazing miracle in history is the **Incarnation**. This word means "taking on flesh." The God who created the stars became a tiny embryo in the womb of a teenage girl named Mary.

Jesus was not a "ghost" or a God pretending to be a human. He was a real man.

- **He grew tired.** He had to sit down and rest.
- **He got hungry and thirsty.** He asked people for water and food.
- **He felt emotions.** He felt deep joy, and He wept with sorrow when His friend died.
- **He was tempted.** He felt the pull of temptation, yet He never once gave in to sin.

Why did He have to be human? Because humans are the ones who sinned. To be our substitute, Jesus had to be one of us. He had to live the perfect human life that we failed to live.

Two Natures, One Person

Theologians use a fancy term for this: the **Hypostatic Union**. It simply means that Jesus is one Person with two natures. He is 100% God and 100% man at the same time.

Think of it this way:

- As God, He knows everything; as man, He grew in wisdom.
- As God, He sustains the universe; as man, He needed to sleep.

He didn't lose His "God-hood" when He became a man. He just added a human nature to His divine nature. He is the bridge between heaven and earth. Because He is both, He can take the hand of a holy God and the hand of a sinful human and bring them together.

The Three Offices of Jesus

In the Old Testament, God used three main types of leaders to help His people. Jesus came to be the perfect version of all three.

1. The Prophet

A prophet speaks God's words to the people. Jesus didn't just speak God's words; He *is* the Word. He told us the truth about God, life, and the future. When we listen to Jesus, we are hearing exactly what God wants to say to us.

2. The Priest

A priest represents the people before God and offers sacrifices for their sins. Jesus is our Great High Priest. He didn't offer a goat or a lamb; He offered Himself as the final sacrifice. Now, He stands in heaven praying for us and making sure we have access to the Father.

3. The King

A king rules and protects his people. Jesus is the King of kings. He has authority over every atom in the universe. One day, He will return to set up a kingdom where there is no more crying or pain. Right now, He wants to be the King of your heart.

"The Son is the image of the invisible God, the firstborn over all creation." - *Colossians 1:15*

Why This Matters to You

1. God Understands You Because Jesus became a man, God knows what it feels like to be you. He knows what it's like to be tired, stressed, or lonely. He knows the pain of being betrayed by a friend. When you pray, you aren't talking to a distant computer; you are talking to a Savior who has walked in your shoes.

2. You Can See What God Is Like Do you want to know how God feels about people who are hurting? Look at Jesus. Do you want to know how God feels about hypocrisy and pride? Look at Jesus. He is the "visible image of the invisible God." If you know Jesus, you know the Father.

3. He Is the Only Way Because Jesus is the only God-man, He is the only one qualified to bridge the gap caused by sin. No other religious leader or philosophy can do what He did. He is the only one who lived a perfect life and the only one who could pay for our rebellion.

1. Why is it important that Jesus is *fully* God? What would happen to our faith if He were just a "really good man"?

2. Why is it important that Jesus is *fully* human? How does it make you feel to know that He experienced the same struggles you do?

3. If Jesus is the "King" of your life, what is one area where you need to let Him lead you this week?

CHAPTER 9

THE WORK OF THE CROSS

If you walk into a jewelry store at the mall, you will likely see a whole section dedicated to crosses. You can buy them in gold, silver, or covered in diamonds. You see them printed on t-shirts, tattooed on arms, and placed on top of church steeples. The cross has become the most recognized symbol of the Christian faith. It is so common that we often forget what it actually is.

In the ancient Roman world, the cross was not a piece of fashion. It was a tool of terror. It was an instrument of torture designed to kill a person as slowly and painfully as possible. It was reserved for the worst criminals, rebels, and slaves. For a Roman citizen, the very idea of crucifixion was so shameful that they would not even speak of it in polite society.

So, why do Christians cherish this symbol? Why do we sing songs about it? Why do we call the day Jesus died "Good Friday"? The answer is that the cross is the turning point of history. It is where the holy justice of God and the infinite love of God collided. To understand Christianity, you must understand what happened on that hill outside of Jerusalem. It was not just a martyrdom; it was a rescue mission.

The Cup of Wrath

To understand the cross, we have to go back to the Garden of Gethsemane. This happened the night before Jesus died. The Bible tells us that Jesus was in agonizing pain. He was so stressed that He sweat drops of blood. He prayed a very specific prayer: "Going a little farther, he fell with his face to the ground and prayed, "My Father, if it is possible, may this cup be taken from me. Yet not as I will, but as you will." (Matthew 26:39)

What was in the "cup"? Was Jesus afraid of the physical pain? Surely, He knew the nails would hurt. But many martyrs throughout history have died bravely, singing hymns while they were burned at the stake. Jesus was afraid of something far worse than physical death.

In the Old Testament, the "cup" is often a symbol of God's wrath. It represents the anger of a holy God against sin. Imagine a cup filled with every lie, every hateful thought, every act of selfishness, and every moment of pride. Now add the sins of every person who has ever lived. God, because He is good, hates this evil. Justice demands a penalty. That is what was in the cup. Jesus was about to drink that cup down to the dregs, experiencing the full weight of judgment for us.

The Great Exchange

Theologians call what happened on the cross **Penal Substitutionary Atonement**. That is a mouthful, but the concept is simple and beautiful.

- **Penal:** It involves a legal penalty or punishment.
- **Substitutionary:** Jesus took our place.
- **Atonement:** The broken relationship is fixed; we are made "at one" with God.

Think of it as a "Great Exchange." Imagine you are standing in a courtroom. You have a stack of treason accusations against the King. You are guilty. Suddenly, the King's Son walks in. He has a perfect record. He looks at the judge and says, "I will take his punishment. Put his crimes on my record, and give him my freedom."

On the cross, God treated Jesus as if He had lived your life. He was punished for your mistakes. In exchange, God treats you as if you had lived Jesus' life. You get His perfect score. This is why the cross is the only way to be saved. We cannot pay our own debt. Only Jesus could pay it.

Four Words That Change Everything

When we talk about the work of the cross, the Bible uses four key words to describe what Jesus accomplished. Each word gives us a different angle on the diamond of salvation.

1. **Propitiation (Satisfying the Anger)** God is holy. His holiness burns against sin like fire burns up paper. Jesus offered Himself as the sacrifice that absorbed that fire. Because of the cross, God's wrath toward believers is exhausted. There is none left for you. When God looks at you now, He is not angry; He is pleased.

2. **Redemption (Buying Freedom)** This word comes from the ancient slave markets. If a person was a slave, someone could pay a "ransom" to buy their freedom. The Bible says we were slaves to sin. Jesus paid the ransom price. The cost was not silver or gold; it was His own blood. You belong to God now because He bought you back.

3. **Justification (Legal Standing)** This is a legal term. It is the opposite of condemnation. It doesn't just mean "innocent", it means "righteous." Because Jesus gave you His record, you are legally righteous in God's eyes. It is "just as if" you never sinned.

4. **Reconciliation (Restoring Friendship)** Sin did not just break a law; it broke a relationship. It made us enemies of God. The cross is the peace treaty. It removed the barrier of sin that stood between us and God. Now, we are not just citizens; we are friends and family.

"It Is Finished"

Toward the end of His time on the cross, Jesus shouted one final word in Greek: *Tetelestai*. We translate this as "It is finished." In those days, this word was often written on tax receipts. It meant "Paid in Full."

Jesus was not admitting defeat. He was shouting a victory cry. He was declaring that the work of salvation was complete. The debt of sin was zeroed out. At that moment, the thick curtain in the Temple that separated people from God's presence tore in two from top to bottom. God tore it. He was showing the world that the barrier was gone. Because the debt was paid, we can now come into the presence of a holy God without fear.

"For Christ also suffered once for sins, the righteous for the unrighteous, to bring you to God. He was put to death in the body but made alive in the Spirit." - 1 Peter 3:18

1. **You Do Not Have to Pay** Many of us live with a low-level sense of guilt. We feel like we need to "make up" for our mistakes. The cross tells us that the debt is already paid. You cannot add to His payment. You are free to obey God out of love and gratitude, not out of fear or guilt.

2. **You Are Defined by Love** How do you know someone loves you? You look at what they are willing to sacrifice for you. God did not wait for you to get your act together; He died for you while you were still a sinner. When you feel worthless, look at the cross. It is God's proof of how much He wants you.

3. **You Have a Safe Anchor** Life is shaky, and feelings change. But the work of the cross is a historical fact. Your standing with God does not depend on how good you feel today; it depends on what Jesus did 2,000 years ago. That is a rock you can build your life on.

Reflect and Talk

1. Why is it important to understand that the "cup" Jesus drank was not just physical death, but spiritual judgment?

2. If someone asked you, "How can one man pay for the sins of the whole world?", how would you use the concept of the "Great Exchange" to explain it?

3. Which of the four words (Propitiation, Redemption, Justification, Reconciliation) makes you feel the most grateful today? Why?

CHAPTER 10

OUR ADVOCATE (THE HOLY SPIRIT)

If you have ever tried to follow Jesus on your own strength, you probably realized pretty quickly that it is hard. You might start the day with great intentions, but by lunchtime, you've lost your temper, or you've let a selfish thought take over. It can feel like trying to drive a car with no gasoline, you can steer it and polish it, but it isn't going anywhere.

The good news is that God never intended for you to live the Christian life alone. Before Jesus went to the cross, He told His disciples something shocking: He said: "But very truly I tell you, it is for your good that I am going away. Unless I go away, the Advocate will not come to you; but if I go, I will send him to you." (John 16:7). That is the Holy Spirit. He is not a "vibe," a "feeling," or a ghostly mist; He is the third Person of the Trinity, and He is the power source for your life.

Who Is the Holy Spirit?

As we learned in the chapter on the Trinity, the Holy Spirit is fully God. He isn't a "junior partner" in the Godhead, nor is He "lesser" than the Father or the Son. He has a mind, emotions, and a will. The Bible tells us: "And do not grieve the Holy Spirit of God, with whom you were sealed for the day of redemption." (Ephesians 4:30)

In the Old Testament, the Holy Spirit would "come upon" specific people for specific tasks, like giving King Solomon wisdom or giving an artist the skill to build the Tabernacle. But after Jesus rose from the dead and went to heaven, something radical happened. On the day of Pentecost, the Holy Spirit was poured out on *all* believers. Now, if you belong to Jesus, the Holy Spirit doesn't just visit you; He lives inside you.

The Spotlight: The Spirit's Main Mission

One of the most important things to understand about the Holy Spirit is that He is humble. He doesn't seek the limelight. Theologians often describe His work as a "floodlight ministry." If you walk past a beautiful monument at night, you don't stare at the floodlights on the ground; you look at the monument they are shining on.

The Holy Spirit's primary mission is to point to Jesus. He helps you understand the Bible, reminds you of God's promises, and makes the person of Jesus feel "real" to you. When you suddenly feel a deep sense of love for God or a clear understanding of a Bible verse, that isn't just your brain working, that is the Holy Spirit shining His spotlight on the truth.

The Work of the Spirit: Conviction and New Life

The Holy Spirit's work starts before you even become a Christian. He is the one who "opens your eyes." Without His help, the things of God seem like foolishness to us.

1. Regeneration (New Birth)

The Bible says that because of sin, our spirits were "dead." We couldn't fix ourselves. The Holy Spirit is the one who performs "spiritual CPR." He breathes life into our souls. This is what Jesus meant by being "born again." The Spirit changes our hearts of stone into hearts of flesh that actually want to love God.

2. Conviction

Have you ever done something wrong and felt a sudden "tug" or "heavy weight" in your heart? That isn't just a bad feeling; it is the Holy Spirit. He "convicts" us of sin. He isn't doing this to shame us or make us feel like garbage. He does it because He loves us. He shows us the truth about our sin so that we will turn back to the Father for forgiveness. He is like a doctor pointing out a sickness so that He can provide the cure.

The Internal Power Source: Sanctification

Once the Holy Spirit moves in, He begins a lifelong project called **Sanctification**. This is the process of making you more like Jesus. It is a partnership: you choose to obey, but the Spirit provides the power to actually do it.

The Fruit of the Spirit

You cannot "force" yourself to be a truly joyful or patient person any more than an apple tree can "force" itself to grow apples. Growth comes from the "sap" inside. When you stay connected to God, the Holy Spirit produces "fruit" in your life: love, joy, peace, patience, kindness, goodness, faithfulness, gentleness, and self-control (Galatians 5:22-23). These aren't just personality traits; they are the character of Jesus being grown inside of you.

Power Over Temptation

On your own, you might give in to temptation every time. But the Bible says: "And if the Spirit of him who raised Jesus from the dead is living in you, he who raised Christ from the dead will also give life to your mortal bodies because of his Spirit who lives in you." (Romans 8:11) This means you have access to supernatural strength. When you feel a temptation to lie or to be greedy, you can ask the Holy Spirit for help. He provides the "way of escape" and the strength to say "no."

Spiritual Gifts: Tools for the Family

The Holy Spirit doesn't just give you "fruit" (character); He also gives you "gifts" (abilities). Every single believer is given at least one spiritual gift. These aren't for showing off; they are "tools" given to help the Church.

- **Communication Gifts:** Like teaching, encouragement, or sharing the Gospel.
- **Service Gifts:** Like helping others, being generous, or leadership.
- **Support Gifts:** Like wisdom, faith, or showing mercy to those who are hurting.

The Spirit decides who gets which gift. You don't have to be jealous of someone else's gift, and you shouldn't feel useless because you don't have theirs. You are like a piece of a puzzle; the Holy Spirit has given you exactly what you need to help the "Big Picture" of God's plan.

The Seal and the Guarantee

In the ancient world, when a king sent a letter, he would melt wax on the envelope and press his signet ring into it. This was a "seal." It proved who owned the letter and guaranteed it wouldn't be messed with.

The Bible says the Holy Spirit is God's "seal" on your life (Ephesians 1:13-14). He is also called a "deposit" or a "guarantee." When the Holy Spirit moves into your heart, He is God's way of saying, "This person belongs to Me, and I am going to finish the work I started." He is the down payment on the eternal life you will one day have in heaven.

"The Spirit himself testifies with our spirit that we are God's children." - *Romans 8:16*

Walking by the Spirit

How do we actually interact with the Holy Spirit? The Bible uses the phrase "Walk by the Spirit."

Walking is a slow, steady, step-by-step process. It means staying in constant communication with Him.

- **Listening:** We listen to the Spirit by reading the Bible, because the Spirit is the one who inspired the authors to write it. He will never tell you to do something that contradicts the Bible.

- **Surrendering:** It means saying, "Not my will, but Yours." When you feel that nudge to apologize to a friend, or to spend time praying instead of scrolling on your phone, that is an invitation to walk with Him.

- **Depending:** It means admitting, "Holy Spirit, I can't do this today without You. Please give me Your patience and Your love."

Why This Matters to You

1. You are Never Truly Alone One of the titles Jesus gave the Holy Spirit is "The Comforter." When you feel lonely, misunderstood, or abandoned, remember that God Himself lives within you. He is closer to you than your own breath. You have a constant Friend who knows your thoughts and feels your pain.

2. You Don't Have to Be "Perfect" Today The Christian life isn't about you trying harder to be good so that God will love you. It's about you being loved by God and letting the Holy Spirit change you from the inside out. You can stop stressing about your performance and start trusting His power.

3. You Have a Purpose and the Power to Fulfill It Do you feel like you have nothing to offer? The Holy Spirit disagrees. He has placed specific gifts in you that the world needs. Because He is in you, you can do things you never thought possible—like forgiving someone who deeply hurt you, or finding peace in the middle of a massive life storm.

Reflect and Talk

1. Why is it more comforting to know the Holy Spirit is a *Person* you can have a relationship with, rather than just an "energy" or a "power source"?

2. Look at the list of the Fruit of the Spirit in Galatians 5:22-23. Which of those do you see the Holy Spirit growing in you right now? Which one do you feel you need the most help with this week?

3. How does the idea of the Holy Spirit being a "seal" or a "guarantee" change how you feel about your security in God?

SECTION FIVE
THE GIFT

SAVED BY GRACE ALONE

Imagine you are deep underwater, far below the surface where the light can't reach. Your lungs are burning, you are out of oxygen, and you are completely unable to swim back up on your own. You don't need a "how-to" manual on swimming. You don't need someone to give you a pep talk about trying harder. You need someone to dive in, grab you, and pull you to the surface. You need a rescue.

This is the heart of the doctrine of **Grace**. In the previous chapters, we looked at how great God is and how broken we are. Now we ask the most important question: *How does a person get right with God?* The answer isn't "try harder" or "be better." The answer is a single word: Grace.

Grace vs. Mercy vs. Justice

To understand grace, we have to distinguish it from two other words we often use in church.

- **Justice** is getting what you *do* deserve. (If you break the law and get a fine, that's justice.)

- **Mercy** is *not* getting what you *do* deserve. (If you break the law but the judge lets you off without the fine, that's mercy.)

- **Grace** is getting what you *do not* deserve. (If the judge lets you off the fine and then gives you $1,000 to start over, that's grace.)

In the Gospel, God gives us all three. He satisfies **Justice** by punishing Jesus for our sins. He shows **Mercy** by not punishing us. And He pours out **Grace** by giving us eternal life and adopting us into His family.

The most common mistake people make about Christianity is thinking that it is a "ladder" we climb to get to God. We think if we pray enough, read our Bibles enough, and stay out of trouble, God will finally accept us.

But the Bible says the exact opposite: "David says the same thing when he speaks of the blessedness of the one to whom God credits righteousness apart from works:" (Romans 4:6). This means there is absolutely nothing you can do to make God love you more, and nothing you have done that makes Him love you less.

If you could earn your way into heaven, then Jesus wouldn't have needed to die. If you could be "good enough," then salvation would be a paycheck you earned, not a gift you received. But because salvation is a gift, no one can brag about it.

Faith: The Hand that Receives

If grace is the gift, **Faith** is the hand that reaches out to take it.

Faith is often misunderstood. It isn't just "believing that God exists", even the demons believe that! True faith is **trust**. It is like sitting down in a chair. You don't just "believe" the chair will hold you; you actually put your weight on it.

We are saved when we stop putting our weight on our own "goodness" and put all our weight on what Jesus did on the cross. We stop saying "I am a good person" and start saying "Jesus is a great Savior."

The Five "Solas"

During a time in history called the Reformation, theologians came up with five Latin phrases (the "Solas") to protect the true meaning of grace. They serve as guardrails to keep us from falling into the trap of thinking we save ourselves.

1. **Sola Gratia (Grace Alone):** We are saved only by God's unmerited favor.
2. **Sola Fide (Faith Alone):** We receive this salvation only through trust, not by doing chores for God.

3. **Solus Christus (Christ Alone):** Jesus is the only bridge between us and the Father.

4. **Sola Scriptura (Scripture Alone):** The Bible is our only final authority for how to be saved.

5. **Soli Deo Gloria (Glory to God Alone):** Since God did all the work, He gets 100% of the credit.

> **"For it is by grace you have been saved, through faith—and this is not from yourselves, it is the gift of God— not by works, so that no one can boast." - *Ephesians 2:8-9***

Grace is Not a License to Sin

Whenever you talk about "Grace Alone," someone always asks: "If I'm saved by grace and not by being good, does that mean I can just go out and sin all I want?"

The Apostle Paul answered: "By no means! We are those who have died to sin; how can we live in it any longer?" (Romans 6:2)

Think of it this way: If someone jumped into a freezing river and saved you from drowning at the cost of their own health, you wouldn't say, "Great! Now I'm going to go throw rocks at their house!" You would love them. You would want to do anything for them because you are so grateful.

Works are the *result* of salvation, not the *cause* of it. We don't do good things *to get* saved; we do good things because we *are* saved. Obedience is our "thank you" note to God.

Why This Matters to You

1. You Can Stop Performing Many teens feel a massive amount of pressure to be perfect, to have the best grades, the best body, or the best social media feed. Grace is the only place in the world where the pressure is off. You don't have to perform for God. You are already loved, accepted, and "righteous" in His eyes because of Jesus.

2. You Can Be Honest About Your Mess If you believe you are saved by being "good," you will always try to hide your mistakes. But if you are saved by grace, you can be honest. You can admit when you're struggling, because you know your standing with God isn't based on your perfection.

3. It Gives You a Heart for Others When you realize that you are a "beggar who found bread," you stop being judgmental toward other people. You realize that you aren't "better" than the person who doesn't know God; you're just a person who has been rescued by a very kind Savior.

1. Why is it so hard for us to accept a "free gift"? Why do we always want to pay God back or prove we are worthy?

2. If you knew for 100% certainty that God's love for you would never change regardless of your performance, how would that change your stress levels this week?

3. How would you explain the difference between "Grace" and "Justice" to a friend who thinks they have to be "good enough" for God?

CHAPTER 12

REPENTANCE AND FAITH

Imagine you are driving down a long, straight highway at night. You're making great time, your favorite music is playing, and you feel completely in control. But then, you pass a road sign that glows under your headlights, and your heart sinks. You realize you've been driving North for the last hour when your destination is actually South.

What do you do? You don't just keep driving and hope the road eventually circles back. You don't just slow down to 20 mph to "sin less" while still heading the wrong way. To get where you need to be, you have to do something decisive: you have to stop the car, find a place to turn around, and head in the opposite direction.

In the Bible, this "U-turn" is the only proper response to the grace of God. It consists of two inseparable actions: **Repentance** and **Faith**. Theologians often call these the "two wings of an airplane" or "two sides of a coin." You cannot have one without the other. If you try to have faith without repentance, you're just adding Jesus to your old life. If you try to have repentance without faith, you're just trying to fix yourself without a Savior.

Repentance: More Than Just "I'm Sorry"

The word "repentance" often gets a bad reputation in our culture. We picture a sidewalk preacher shouting at people, or someone groveling in the dirt feeling miserable. But the biblical word for repentance is *metanoia*, which literally means "a change of mind." It's an intellectual, emotional, and volitional shift.

It is vital to distinguish between **Biblical Repentance** and **Worldly Regret**.

- **Regret** is being sorry you got caught. It's the feeling you get when you see the police lights in your rearview mirror. It is focused on *consequences*.

- **Repentance** is being sorry for the sin itself because it offends a holy God. It is focused on *character*.

True repentance involves three distinct layers:

1. Your Mind (Intellectual)

You stop making excuses for your behavior. You stop saying, "Well, I only lied because they started it," or "Everyone else is doing it." You agree with God that your sin is a rebellion against Him. You change your mind about who is the boss of your life.

2. Your Heart (Emotional)

The Bible calls this "godly sorrow." It's a deep grief over the fact that your sin has wounded the heart of the God who loves you and died for you. It's not a shame that makes you want to hide (like Adam and Eve in the bushes); it's a sorrow that makes you want to run *to* God for help.

3. Your Will (Volitional)

This is the action. You make a deliberate choice to turn away from the sin and turn toward God. It's like realizing you are holding a handful of poisonous snakes and dropping them immediately. You don't drop them because you're trying to earn a "Good Person" award; you drop them because you realize they are killing you and those around you.

Faith: The Anchor of the Soul

If repentance is the "turning away," then faith is the "turning to." As we touched on in the previous chapter, saving faith is far more than just "believing that God exists." The Bible tells us that even the demons believe God exists—and they tremble in fear (James 2:19).

Theologians describe three essential layers of faith that must work together:

- **Knowledge (*Notitia*):** You have to know the facts. You cannot have faith in a Jesus you've never heard of. You must know that He lived, died for sins, and rose again.

- **Agreement (*Assensus*):** You have to believe those facts are true. You agree that the Bible is accurate and that Jesus is indeed the Son of God.

- **Trust (*Fiducia*):** This is the "spark" of saving faith. This is when you personally rely on Jesus to save *you*.

Think of it like a chair. You can have the **knowledge** of how a chair is built. You can **agree** that the chair looks sturdy enough to hold a person. But you don't actually have "faith" in that chair until you put all your weight on it and lift your feet off the ground. Faith is "putting your weight" on the finished work of Jesus and trusting Him with your eternal destiny.

The Great Tug-of-War: The Coin with Two Sides

You cannot truly turn *to* God (Faith) without turning *away* from your old life (Repentance). Imagine you are holding a heavy bag of trash in your right hand. Someone stands before you and offers you a bar of solid gold. To reach out and take the gold, you *must* let go of the trash.

- **Repentance** is the act of letting go of the trash.
- **Faith** is the act of reaching out for the gold.

If you say you have "faith" but you refuse to let go of your secret sins or your desire to be your own god, your hands are too full to receive the gift Jesus is offering. Conversely, if you just "drop the trash" but never reach for Jesus, you're just a person standing in a mess with empty hands.

A Gift, Not a Work

One of the most mind-blowing things about theology is that even our ability to repent and believe is a gift from God.

If we are "dead in our sins" (as we learned in Chapter 7), a dead person cannot decide to wake up and have faith. God has to perform a miracle in our hearts first. He gives us the "eyes to see" how beautiful Jesus is and "ears to hear" the truth of the Gospel.

This keeps us humble. We can't get to heaven and brag, "I was smart enough to repent!" Instead, we say, "Thank You, God, for opening my eyes so I could see that I needed to turn around."

"The time has come," he said. "The kingdom of God has come near. Repent and believe the good news!" - *Mark 1:15*

1. It's a Lifestyle, Not a One-Time Event Many people think repentance is something you do once to "get saved" and then you're done. But Martin Luther, a famous reformer, said that the entire life of a believer should be one of repentance. Following Jesus means that every day, we realize we've drifted off course, and every day, we turn back to Him. It's a lifestyle of honesty and "refreshing" your soul.

2. It Offers a Constant Fresh Start No matter how far you have driven in the wrong direction, a U-turn is always available. God's grace is bigger than your biggest failure. When you come to God in repentance, He doesn't say, "I told you so." He doesn't hold a grudge. He says, "Welcome home," and He wipes the slate clean.

3. It Removes the Pressure of "Strong Faith" Many teens worry, "Is my faith strong enough?" But here is the secret: It isn't the *strength* of your faith that saves you; it is the *Object* of your faith. Imagine two people crossing a frozen lake. One has "strong faith" and runs across confidently. The other has "weak faith" and crawls across trembling. If the ice is thick, both are safe. If the ice is thin, the confident person falls in just as fast as the trembling person. Our "ice" is Jesus. He is solid. Even if your faith feels small and shaky, if it is placed in a strong Savior, you are 100% secure.

1. Why do you think people are often afraid of the word "Repentance"? How does the "U-turn" illustration make it feel more hopeful?

2. Looking at the three layers of faith (Knowledge, Agreement, Trust), which one do you think is the hardest for people your age to grasp?

3. Is there something in your life right now that feels like "trash" you need to let go of so you can reach out for the "gold" of God's grace?

CHAPTER 13

ADOPTED INTO THE FAMILY

Imagine for a moment that you are an orphan living on the streets of a massive, indifferent city. You have no last name, no bank account, and no one to look out for you. You are constantly worried about where your next meal will come from and where you will sleep. You are "invisible" to the world, just another person trying to survive.

Then, one day, the King of the country pulls up in his carriage. He doesn't just give you some spare change or a warm meal to keep you going for another night. He doesn't even just offer you a job in the palace kitchens. Instead, he brings you into his private study, signs a legal document with his royal seal, and says, "From now on, you are my child. You carry my name. My home is your home. Everything I have belongs to you."

In theology, we call this **Adoption**. While "Justification" is a legal term that says you are "not guilty" in the eyes of the law, Adoption is a relational term that says you are "home." It is the highest privilege the Gospel offers. It takes us from the courtroom of the Judge to the living room of the Father.

The Great Shift: From Enemy to Heir

To understand how massive this deal is, we have to remember where we started. Because of sin, the Bible doesn't describe us as "natural" children of God. In our culture, people often say, "We are all children of God." While it's true that we are all *creatures* made by God, the Bible is very specific that we are only *children* through Jesus. Before we met Christ, the Bible says: "Once you were alienated from God and were enemies in your minds because of your evil behavior." (Colossians 1:21). We weren't just "lost"; we were on the other side of a war.

When God saves us, He does something far beyond just pardoning our crimes. He brings us into the inner circle. He doesn't just let us into heaven as "guests" who have to stay in the lobby, or "servants" who work the grounds. He makes us family.

1. A New Status (The Name)

In the ancient world, adoption was a serious legal matter. When a child was adopted, their old debts were wiped out, and they received a new family name. They gained a new identity that could never be taken away. You are now a son or daughter of the Most High. This isn't just a title; it is the core of who you are.

2. A New Standing (The Access)

Think about the difference between a servant and a child. A servant has to knock, wait for permission, and enter the King's room with their head bowed, hoping they aren't interrupting. A child just walks in. A child can run into the Father's room at 3:00 AM because they had a bad dream, and the Father won't be angry, He'll open His arms. "In him and through faith in him we may approach God with freedom and confidence" (Ephesians 3:12).

3. A New Future (The Inheritance)

In ancient times, the "heir" was the one who inherited the father's entire estate. The Bible says we are "heirs of God and fellow heirs with Christ" (Romans 8:17). Stop and think about that for a second. Everything that belongs to Jesus, His joy, His victory, His closeness to the Father, His authority over the new creation, is shared with you. You aren't just getting a "ticket to heaven"; you are inheriting a Kingdom.

The Spirit of Adoption: The Inner Whisper

How do we know we are actually God's children? Is it just a legal theory written in a book somewhere? No. God gives us an internal "witness."

The Bible says that God has sent the "Spirit of adoption" into our hearts. This Spirit helps us cry out, *"Abba, Father!"* (Galatians 4:6). *Abba* is an Aramaic word that is very personal. It's a bit like a child saying "Papa" or "Dad" or "Dada." It's a term of deep, gut-level affection and trust.

The Holy Spirit works in us in two ways regarding our adoption:

First, He Assures Us. On your worst days, when you feel like a failure or when you feel like God must be disappointed in you, the Holy Spirit whispers to your heart, "You are still His. You are still a child." He reminds you that your position in the family isn't based on your performance but on the Father's promise.

Second, He Changes Us. The Spirit helps you start looking like your Father. Just like you might have your dad's eyes, your mom's laugh, or your grandfather's sense of humor, the Spirit helps you develop God's "family traits." You start to value what He values. You start to love people you used to ignore. You start to find joy in things that used to seem boring. This is the "family likeness" growing in you.

The Discipline of a Father: Proof of Love

Being adopted into God's family doesn't mean life is always easy or that you get everything you want. In fact, sometimes it feels like God is being "hard" on you. This can be confusing unless you understand the heart of a father.

Hebrews 12 tells us not to be discouraged when we face trials, because "the Lord disciplines the one he loves." Think about it this way: If you see a random kid at the park throwing a tantrum or being mean to others, you probably won't step in and correct him. Why? Because he's not your kid. You might think it's sad, but it's not your responsibility. But if your *own* child acts that way, you step in immediately. You might take away a toy, give them a "time out," or have a serious talk. You do this because you love them too much to let them grow up to be a jerk.

When God allows us to go through hard times or "corrects" our behavior through a guilty conscience or difficult circumstances, it is actually proof that we belong to Him. He isn't "punishing" us (Jesus already took our punishment on the cross); He is **training** us. He is pruning us so we can grow better. A good father cares more about his child's character than his child's comfort.

The Family Business: Representing the King

When you are adopted into a royal family, you don't just sit in the palace and eat grapes all day. You represent the family. You enter the "family business."

Our family business is the **Kingdom of God**. As children of the King, we are now ambassadors. We represent His interests on earth.

- **We Care What He Cares About:** We care about justice, mercy, and truth because our Father does. We stand up for the bullied and the broken because our Father is a "Father to the fatherless."

- **We Love the Other Kids:** Being adopted by God means you are also adopted into a massive, global family. Every other believer is your brother or sister. This means we treat other Christians with kindness and forgiveness, even when they are difficult, because we share the same Father.

- **We Invite Others In:** Our mission is to go back to the streets where we used to live and tell the other "orphans" that there is a King who wants to adopt them too. We aren't better than them; we're just kids who found a Father.

Why This Matters to You

1. Your Identity is Unshakeable In the ancient Roman world, an adoption was actually more permanent than a natural birth. Under Roman law, a father could disown a biological son, but a son who was *legally adopted* could never be disowned. God chose you. He knew exactly what He was getting when He brought you into the family. He knew your future mistakes and your hidden struggles, and He signed the papers anyway. You can rest in the fact that your place in the family is secure.

2. You Don't Have to Fear the Future If the King of the universe is your Dad, what do you really have to be afraid of? Stress about school, worries about what people think of you, and fears about the future all start to shrink when you realize the person in charge of the universe loves you as His own child. He has promised to provide for you and to never leave you.

3. You Have Total Access You don't need a priest, a "professional" Christian, or a perfect prayer life to talk to God. You are His child. You can go to Him with your smallest worries, like a test you're nervous about, and your biggest fears. He is never too busy for you, He never thinks your problems are "stupid," and He never grows tired of hearing your voice.

"See what great love the Father has lavished on us, that we should be called children of God! And that is what we are! The reason the world does not know us is that it did not know him." - *1 John 3:1*

1. What is the difference between thinking of God as a "Boss" and thinking of Him as a "Father"? How does that change the way you pray tonight?

2. If you truly believed that you were an "heir" of everything God owns, how would that change the way you feel when you feel "less than" or "not enough" at school?

3. How does knowing that God's discipline is a sign of *love* change how you look at the "rough patches" or "nos" you've received from Him lately?

SECTION SIX

THE NEW LIFE

CHAPTER 14

GROWING TO BE LIKE JESUS

Once you have been rescued by grace and adopted into God's family, a new question naturally pops up: *What now?* If you've ever watched a baby grow, you know it's a process. They don't walk the day they are born. They don't speak full sentences for a long time. But day by day, as they eat, sleep, and interact with their parents, they start to change. They start to look and act more like the family they belong to.

In theology, the word for this "growing up" process is **Sanctification**. While justification is God's work of declaring you "right" in a single moment, sanctification is God's work of making you "holy" over a lifetime. It is the journey of the "Old You" (the one ruled by sin) slowly being replaced by the "New You" (the one who looks like Jesus).

The Two Natures: A House Under Renovation

Imagine you buy a house that is falling apart. The roof leaks, the walls are covered in mold, and the foundation is cracked. When God saves you, He "buys" the house. But He doesn't just leave it that way. He moves in and starts a massive renovation project.

As a Christian, you often feel a "tug-of-war" inside you. The Apostle Paul described this in Romans 7. Part of you wants to love God and do what is right, but another part of you, which the Bible calls "the flesh", still wants to go back to your old ways.

- **The Flesh:** The leftover habits, desires, and selfishness of your old life.

- **The Spirit:** The new life God has placed in you that desires to please Him.

Sanctification is the process of "starving" the flesh and "feeding" the Spirit. It is not about being "perfect" today; it is about being more like Jesus today than you were yesterday.

Growth doesn't happen by accident, and it doesn't happen just by trying harder. An apple tree doesn't grow fruit by "gritting its teeth." It grows fruit by staying connected to the roots and getting sunlight and water. We grow by using the **Means of Grace**—the tools God has given us to stay connected to Him.

1. The Word of God (The Bible)

If you want to look like Jesus, you have to know what Jesus is like. The Bible is more than just a history book; it is "living and active." As you read it, the Holy Spirit uses it to rewire your brain, changing the way you think about yourself, others, and the world.

2. Prayer (The Connection)

Prayer is the "breath" of the Christian life. It is how we express our dependence on God. When we pray, we aren't just giving God a shopping list of things we want; we are aligning our hearts with His. We are asking Him for the strength to do what we can't do on our own.

3. Fellowship (The Community)

As we learned earlier, you cannot grow to be like Jesus in isolation. You need other Christians to encourage you, challenge you, and help you see the blind spots in your life. We are like "living stones" being built together.

4. Worship and Sacraments

Participating in the life of the church, singing together, taking communion, and witnessing baptisms, reminds us of the "Big Story" we are a part of. It pulls our focus off our own problems and puts it back on God's glory.

The Goal: The Fruit of the Spirit

What does a "grown-up" Christian actually look like? It's not necessarily someone who has the most Bible verses memorized or someone who never makes a mistake. A person who is growing like Jesus is someone whose life is increasingly filled with the **Fruit of the Spirit** (Galatians 5:22-23).

Note that the Bible says "fruit" (singular), not "fruits." They are like a single cluster of grapes. God wants to grow *all* of them in you:

- **Love** that puts others first.
- **Joy** that doesn't depend on your circumstances.
- **Peace** that stays calm even when life is messy.
- **Patience** with people who are difficult.
- **Kindness and Goodness** in how you treat everyone.
- **Faithfulness** to your word and your God.
- **Gentleness and Self-Control** over your temper and your desires.

Progress, Not Perfection

One of the biggest traps for Christian teens is **Legalism**. This is the belief that God only likes you if you are performing well. When you fall back into an old sin or have a "bad day," legalism tells you that you've lost God's favor.

But sanctification is a marathon, not a sprint. There will be days when you stumble. There will be seasons where you feel like you're taking two steps forward and one step back.

The key is "Direction, not Perfection." Are you heading toward Jesus? When you fall, do you get back up and run toward Him, or do you stay in the dirt? God is the one doing the work in you, and He is very patient.

"being confident of this, that he who began a good work in you will carry it on to completion until the day of Christ Jesus." - *Philippians 1:6*

Why This Matters to You

1. You Have a New Power Source You don't have to change yourself. You can't! The Holy Spirit is the one who produces the fruit. Your job is to "abide"—to stay close to Jesus. When you stop trying to "act" like a Christian and start "being" with Christ, the change happens naturally.

2. Your Life Gains Meaning Every situation you face, even the hard ones, is an opportunity to grow. A boring day at school is a chance to practice patience. A conflict with a friend is a chance to practice forgiveness. Nothing in your life is wasted because God is using everything to shape you into the image of His Son.

3. You Can Be Patient with Yourself You are a "work in progress." You don't have to have it all figured out yet. You can be honest about your struggles because you know that God isn't finished with you. He is a Master Artist, and He takes His time with His masterpieces.

1. Why is it easier to try to "act" like a Christian (legalism) than to actually "grow" into one (sanctification)?

2. Looking at the Fruit of the Spirit, which one do you feel is most "in season" in your life right now? Which one feels like it's still just a tiny bud?

3. How does the promise in Philippians 1:6 (that God will *finish* the work) help you when you feel like you aren't changing fast enough?

CHAPTER 15

WHY WE NEED THE CHURCH

In the modern world, we love the idea of being "self-made." We have "DIY" projects, solo playlists, and the ability to order anything we want without ever talking to a human being. Many people bring this same "Lone Ranger" attitude to their faith. They say things like, "I love Jesus, but I don't need the church," or "I can worship God just as well on a hike as I can in a building."

While it's true that you can pray anywhere, the Bible knows nothing of a "solitary Christian." To follow Jesus without being part of a church is like trying to be a soldier without an army, a player without a team, or a finger without a body. In this chapter, we look at why the church isn't just a "good idea"; it's essential for your spiritual survival.

The Body of Christ: You Are a Part, Not the Whole

The most famous description of the church is found in 1 Corinthians 12, where the Apostle Paul calls it the **Body of Christ**.

Imagine a human body. It isn't just one giant eyeball or one massive foot. It is made of many parts, hands, ears, lungs, and toes, all doing different jobs.

- **The Diversity:** Every member is different. Some are "loud" parts of the body (like teachers or singers), and some are "quiet" parts (like the people who set up chairs or pray in secret).

- **The Necessity:** A hand is a wonderful thing, but if it is cut off from the body, it loses its purpose and its life. It can't do anything on its own.

- **The Unity:** If your toe gets stubbed, your whole body feels it. In the church, when one person hurts, we all hurt. When one person succeeds, we all celebrate.

If you want to know how God expects you to live, just look at the New Testament. It contains over 50 "one another" commands.

- **Love** one another.
- **Forgive** one another.
- **Pray** for one another.
- **Encourage** one another.
- **Carry** one another's burdens.

Here is the thing: You cannot "one another" yourself. You can't practice forgiveness if you're alone in the woods. You can't carry someone's burden if you don't know anyone's problems. The church is the "gym" where we exercise our spiritual muscles. It is the place where we learn to love people who are different from us, which is exactly how we grow to be like Jesus.

Protection: The Power of the Flock

The Bible often calls God's people a "flock" and Jesus the "Great Shepherd." If you've ever watched a nature documentary, you know that predators (like lions or wolves) don't attack the center of the herd. They wait for the one sheep that thinks it knows better and wanders off on its own.

The church provides three types of protection:

1. **Safety from False Teaching:** When you are alone, it's easy to get confused by weird ideas or bad theology. In a church, you have pastors and older Christians to help you stay grounded in the truth.

2. **Safety from Temptation:** Sin grows in the dark. When we are in community, we have people who can ask us tough questions and keep us accountable.

3. **Safety from Discouragement:** Life is hard. There will be days when your faith feels weak. In those moments, the church "believes for you" until you can find your footing again.

The Means of Grace: A Family Meal

As we learned in the last chapter, we grow through the "Means of Grace." While you can read your Bible and pray alone, there are certain things God only provides when the family gathers.

- **Corporate Worship:** There is a unique power when hundreds of people sing the same truth together. It reminds you that you are part of something much bigger than your own life.

- **The Sacraments:** Baptism and Communion (The Lord's Supper) are "visible words." They are physical reminders of what Jesus did. When we take communion together, we are reminded that we are all equal at the foot of the cross.

- **Preaching:** There is a difference between reading a book and hearing a message "live" that is directed at your community. God uses the preaching of His Word to challenge us in ways we might avoid when reading on our own.

Wait, What About the Hypocrites?

One of the biggest reasons teens avoid church is because they've seen people act like hypocrites. Maybe you've seen a leader fall into sin, or you've been judged by someone in the pews.

It's important to remember: The church is not a museum for saints; it's a **hospital for sinners**. You don't go to a hospital and get mad because there are sick people there; that's why they are there! Every person in your church, including the pastor, is a "work in progress." If the church were perfect, they wouldn't let you or me in! We stay in the church not because the people are perfect, but because the Savior is.

> **"And let us consider how we may spur one another on toward love and good deeds, 25 not giving up meeting together, as some are in the habit of doing, but encouraging one another—and all the more as you see the Day approaching." - *Hebrews 10:24-25***

1. You Have a Job to Do The church is missing a piece if you aren't there. You have a specific gift, a specific personality, and a specific story that the rest of the body needs. You aren't just there to "consume" a service like you're watching Netflix; you are there to contribute.

2. You Get a Multi-Generational Perspective In school, you spend all day with people your own age. In the church, you get to talk to people who have been following Jesus for 50 years. They have wisdom you don't have yet. You also get to help those younger than you. This "family" structure keeps you from being stuck in your own little bubble.

3. It Prepares You for Heaven Heaven isn't going to be a bunch of people sitting on private clouds. It's going to be a "great multitude from every nation, tribe, and tongue" worshiping together. The church is "Basic Training" for heaven. We are learning how to live in community now so we can enjoy it forever.

Reflect and Talk

1. If the church is a "Body," which part do you feel like you are? Are you a "hand" (helping), a "mouth" (encouraging), or "feet" (going)?

2. Why do you think God chose to make us depend on other people for our spiritual growth instead of just letting us grow on our own?

3. How does thinking of the church as a "hospital" change how you feel when you see someone at church act in a way that isn't like Jesus?

CHAPTER 16

BAPTISM AND THE LORD'S SUPPER

Imagine you are watching a wedding. You see the bride and groom exchange rings. Does the ring *make* them married? Not exactly. They are married because of the vows they made and the legal covenant they signed. However, the ring is a visible sign of that invisible promise. It tells the world who they belong to, and it reminds them of their commitment every time they look at it.

In theology, we call Baptism and the Lord's Supper **Ordinances** (because Jesus *ordained* or commanded them) or **Sacraments**. They are "visible words." They are physical actions, using water, bread, and juice, that act as a giant picture of what Jesus has done in our hearts.

Baptism: The Public Announcement

Baptism is the "starting line" of the Christian life. It is a one-time event where a believer is immersed in or washed with water in the name of the Father, the Son, and the Holy Spirit.

What does it symbolize?

Baptism is like a reenactment of the Gospel. When a person goes under the water, it symbolizes their "death" to their old, sinful life. When they come up out of the water, it symbolizes their "resurrection" to a new life in Christ. It is a way of saying, "The old me is dead and buried; the new me lives for Jesus."

Why do we do it?

1. **Obedience:** Jesus explicitly told His followers to go and make disciples, "baptizing them in the name of the Father and of the Son and of the Holy Spirit" (Matthew 28:19).

2. **Identification:** It is like putting on a team jersey. It tells the world, the church, and the spiritual realm that you are officially "on Team Jesus."

3. **Initiation:** It is the formal way we join the local family of God (the church).

Important Note: Baptism doesn't *save* you. You aren't saved by the water; you are saved by the grace of God through faith. Baptism is the outward sign of the inward change that has already happened.

The Lord's Supper: The Family Meal

While baptism happens once, the Lord's Supper (also called Communion or the Eucharist) is something the church does over and over again. It was started by Jesus during the "Last Supper," the night before He was crucified.

The Elements

- **The Bread:** Jesus said, "This is my body, which is given for you." The bread reminds us of the physical suffering Jesus endured to pay for our sins.

- **The Cup:** Jesus said, "This cup... is the new covenant in my blood." The juice or wine reminds us that Jesus' blood was poured out to wash away our guilt.

What are we doing during Communion?

1. **Look Back (Remembrance):** We remember the historical fact of the cross. We don't let the sacrifice of Jesus become "old news."

2. **Look In (Examination):** The Bible tells us to check our hearts before we eat. We confess any recent sins and ask God to help us live for Him.

3. **Look Around (Unity):** We eat from the same loaf and drink from the same cup to show that we are one family. There is no "VIP section" at the Lord's Table.

4. **Look Forward (Hope):** Jesus said He wouldn't drink of the fruit of the vine again until the Kingdom comes. Every time we take communion, we are practicing for the "Great Banquet" in heaven.

> *"For whenever you eat this bread and drink this cup, you*
> *proclaim the Lord's death until he comes." -*
> **1 Corinthians 11:26**

Why These "Rituals" Matter

You might think, "Why do we need physical stuff? Can't I just think about Jesus in my head?"

God created us with bodies, not just floating brains. He knows that we are forgetful people. He gave us baptism and the Lord's Supper because He wanted us to **see, touch, and taste** the Gospel.

- **Water** reminds us we are clean.

- **Bread** reminds us we are sustained.

- **Wine/Juice** reminds us we are forgiven.

These aren't just empty traditions. When the church gathers to perform these actions, the Holy Spirit works in a special way to nourish our faith and strengthen our bond with each other.

Why This Matters to You

1. It Gives You a "Moment to Point To" There will be days when you feel like a "fake" Christian or you doubt if God really loves you. On those days, you can look back at your baptism. It was a physical, public fact. It serves as an anchor for your soul.

2. It Keeps Your Heart Soft Taking the Lord's Supper regularly forces you to stop and deal with your sin. It's like a weekly "system restart." You can't stay mad at a brother or sister in Christ when you are both kneeling at the same table, receiving the same mercy.

3. It Connects You to History When you take the bread and the cup, you are doing the exact same thing that Christians have done in secret caves, massive cathedrals, and jungle villages for 2,000 years. You are part of an ancient, global family.

Reflect and Talk

1. If baptism is like a "wedding ring," what happens if someone wears the ring but doesn't actually love their spouse? (What happens if someone gets baptized but doesn't actually follow Jesus?)

2. Why do you think Jesus chose *food* (bread and drink) to be the way we remember Him? How is Jesus like food for our souls?

3. Have you been baptized? If not, what is holding you back from making that public announcement of your faith?

CHAPTER 17

TALKING TO GOD

Imagine you are friends with the most brilliant, powerful, and kind person on earth. They have given you their private phone number and told you that you can call them 24/7. They never get tired of your voice, they aren't annoyed by your "small" problems, and they have the power to actually help you with your big ones. You would probably call them all the time, right?

This is exactly what **Prayer** is. Many people think of prayer as a religious ritual, a performance, or a list of "magic words" you have to say perfectly. But at its heart, prayer is simply communication with God. It is the breath of the Christian life. If you don't breathe, you can't live. If you don't pray, your relationship with God will start to feel like a distant memory rather than a living reality.

The Purpose: Presence Over Presents

The biggest mistake we make in prayer is thinking that God is a celestial "vending machine." We put in a prayer and expect a specific "snack" to come out. If we don't get exactly what we asked for, we think the machine is broken.

But the main goal of prayer isn't to get things *from* God; it is to get **God Himself**.

- **Relationship:** Prayer is how we build intimacy with our Father.
- **Alignment:** Prayer isn't about bending God's will to match ours; it's about bending our will to match His.
- **Peace:** It is the "safety valve" for our anxiety. When we pour our hearts out to God, we trade our worries for His peace.

When Jesus' disciples asked Him how to pray, He didn't give them a lecture on theology. He gave them a pattern, often called the **Lord's Prayer** (Matthew 6:9–13). This isn't just a poem to memorize; it's a guideline we can follow for our prayers.

1. **"Our Father in heaven, hallowed be your name":** We start by remembering who God is. He is a loving Father (intimate), but He is also in heaven (powerful). We praise Him for His character before we ask for anything.

2. **"Your kingdom come, your will be done":** we ask that God's plans would happen in our lives, our schools, and our world. We are saying, "You're the King, not me."

3. **"Give us this day our daily bread":** Now we ask for what we need. Note it says "daily", God wants us to depend on Him every day.

4. **"Forgive us our debts...":** We confess our sins and ask for a clean slate. We also ask for help to forgive people who have hurt us.

5. **"Lead us not into temptation...":** We admit we are weak and ask God to protect us from the "traps" of sin and the devil.

If you aren't sure where to start when you close your eyes, many Christians use the acronym **A.C.T.S.** to keep their conversation balanced:

- **A - Adoration:** Tell God what you love about Him (His kindness, His power, His beauty).

- **C - Confession:** Be honest about where you've messed up today and ask for forgiveness.

- **T - Thanksgiving:** Thank Him for specific things He has done (a good grade, a fun time with friends, a sunset).

- **S - Supplication:** A fancy word for "asking." Pray for your needs and the needs of others.

Does God Always Answer?

This is the question everyone asks. The short answer is: **Yes.** But His answer isn't always "Yes."

- **Yes:** When what we ask for aligns with His perfect plan.

- **No:** When we ask for something that would hurt us or others, or doesn't fit His better plan. A good father says "no" to a child who wants to eat candy for dinner.

- **Wait:** Sometimes the timing isn't right. God uses the "wait" to grow our patience and our trust in Him.

Remember: God is a Father, not a butler. He loves you enough to give you what you *would* have asked for if you knew everything He knows.

> **"Do not be anxious about anything, but in every situation,**
> **by prayer and petition, with thanksgiving, present your**
> **requests to God." -** *Philippians 4:6*

Why This Matters to You

1. You Have a Stress-Relief Strategy High school is stressful. Between sports, grades, social drama, and thinking about the future, it's easy to feel overwhelmed. Prayer is where you get to "unload" that baggage. You weren't designed to carry the weight of the world; God was.

2. You Are Never Truly Alone Even when you feel misunderstood by your friends or family, you have Someone who truly "gets" you. You can talk to God in the middle of a test, while you're walking to class, or in your room at night. He is the Friend who is always there.

3. It Changes You The more you talk to God, the more you start to think like Him. Your priorities shift. Things that used to make you angry start to matter less, and things God loves start to matter more. Prayer is the secret to a transformed life.

Reflect and Talk

1. Why do you think we often wait until we are in a "crisis" to pray, instead of talking to God about the small things?

2. Which part of the A.C.T.S. acronym is the easiest for you? Which is the hardest?

3. How does knowing that God sometimes says "No" out of love change the way you feel when you don't get what you prayed for?

SECTION SEVEN

THE UNSEEN AND THE FUTURE

CHAPTER 18

ANGELS AND THE SPIRITUAL WORLD

Have you ever felt like there was more to life than just what you can see, touch, and measure? We live in a world of smartphones, concrete buildings, and biology textbooks. We are taught to trust our five senses. If we can't see it under a microscope or detect it with a telescope, we often assume it isn't there.

But the Bible pulls back the curtain on a reality that is just as real as the chair you are sitting on, yet invisible to the human eye. It tells us that we are surrounded by a spiritual realm: a world of light and darkness, of incredible beauty and intense conflict. At the center of this realm are beings created by God to serve His purposes and protect His people. We call them angels.

To understand the full story of God's Kingdom, we have to understand the "unseen" side of the universe.

What Are Angels?

The word "angel" comes from the Greek word *angelos*, which simply means "messenger." This tells us more about their **job** than their **nature**. By nature, angels are spiritual beings. They don't have physical bodies like we do, they don't get sick, and they don't die. They were created by God before the world was even formed to worship Him and carry out His commands.

1. They Are Not "Cute Babies"

In movies and art, angels are often shown as chubby babies with tiny wings or glowing ladies in white dresses. But in the Bible, when an angel appears to a human, the first thing the angel almost always has to say is: *"Do not be afraid!"* Why? Because they are terrifyingly powerful: "Praise the Lord, you his angels, you mighty ones who do his bidding, who obey his word." (Psalm 103:20). One single angel in the Old Testament was able to defeat an entire army in one night. They are warriors, not ornaments.

2. They Are Not Human

A common misconception is that when good people die, they become angels. The Bible actually says that humans and angels are completely different "species" of creation. In fact, the Bible says that angels are fascinated by us! They "long to look" into the story of the Gospel (1 Peter 1:12). Humans are made in the image of God, and in the future, we will actually have a status that is, in some ways, higher than the angels.

3. They Are Numerous and Organized

The Bible speaks of "thousands upon thousands" and "myriads upon myriads" of angels. They aren't just a random crowd; they seem to have an order. We hear about:

- **Archangels:** Like Michael, who is described as a leader among the heavenly host.

- **Cherubim and Seraphim:** Beings that stay close to the throne of God, crying out "Holy, Holy, Holy!" Their primary job is the direct worship of God's majesty.

What Do Angels Actually Do?

Angels are not "free agents" who wander around doing whatever they want. They are perfectly obedient servants of God. Their work can be divided into four main categories:

Worshiping God

This is their favorite thing to do. In the book of Revelation, we see that the throne of God is surrounded by millions of angels who never stop praising Him. They see God's glory clearly, and their natural response is to sing about it. When we worship God in church, we are actually joining in on a "concert" that the angels have been performing for thousands of years.

Revealing God's Message

Throughout history, God has used angels to deliver big news. An angel told Abraham he would have a son. An angel told Mary she would give birth to Jesus. An angel told the shepherds in the field that the Savior had been born. They are the "Divine Couriers" of the King.

Protecting God's People

This is where the idea of "guardian angels" comes from. While the Bible doesn't explicitly say every person has exactly one assigned angel, it *does* say that angels "encamp around those who fear him" (Psalm 34:7). Also: "Are not all angels ministering spirits sent to serve those who will inherit salvation?" (Hebrews 1:14).

Think of them as "Secret Service" agents. Most of the time, they are working behind the scenes, preventing accidents, warding off spiritual attacks, and strengthening us when we are weak. You will likely get to heaven and realize there were dozens of times an angel protected you from something you didn't even know was a threat.

Executing God's Judgment

Because angels are holy, they hate sin just as much as God does. In the Bible, we see angels used to carry out God's discipline. At the end of time, Jesus says He will send His angels to "gather out of his kingdom all causes of sin and all law-breakers" (Matthew 13:41). They are the guardians of God's justice.

The Dark Side: Fallen Angels and Spiritual Warfare

We cannot talk about the spiritual world without talking about the rebellion that happened there. The Bible tells us that at some point in the past, one of the highest angels, often called Lucifer or Satan, became proud. He didn't want to serve God; he wanted to *be* God.

He led a rebellion, and a third of the angels followed him. These are what we call **demons**.

The Nature of the Enemy

Satan and his demons are real, but we shouldn't be obsessed with them, nor should we ignore them. Here is the truth about our spiritual enemies:

- **They are defeated:** On the cross, Jesus "disarmed the spiritual rulers and authorities" (Colossians 2:15). Satan is like a lion on a leash; he can roar, but he can only go as far as God allows.

- **They are liars:** Jesus called Satan "the father of lies." Their main weapon isn't "scary movie" stuff; it is deception. They want to make you doubt God's love, doubt the Bible, and think that sin will make you happy.

- **They are temporary:** Their time is short, and they know it. Their final destination is already decided.

Spiritual Warfare

Because there is a rebellion going on, we are born into a spiritual war zone. The Apostle Paul tells us that our real fight isn't against people, our teachers, our parents, or our "enemies" at school. "For our struggle is not against flesh and blood, but against the rulers, against the authorities, against the powers of this dark world and against the spiritual forces of evil in the heavenly realms." (Ephesians 6:12)

How do we fight? We don't use physical weapons. We use the **Armor of God**:

- **The Belt of Truth:** Knowing what God says is true.
- **The Breastplate of Righteousness:** Resting in the fact that Jesus made us right with God.
- **The Shield of Faith:** Trusting God when things get hard.
- **The Sword of the Spirit:** Using the Word of God (the Bible) to fight off lies.

The Presence of the Holy Spirit vs. Angels

It is important not to get so excited about angels that we forget about the Holy Spirit. Angels are God's servants, but the Holy Spirit is God Himself.

- An angel might stand *beside* you to protect you.
- The Holy Spirit lives *inside* you to change you.

We don't pray to angels, and we don't worship them. If an angel appeared to you today and you tried to bow down, they would immediately stop you and say, "Worship God!" (Revelation 22:9). Angels are our "fellow servants." They are on our side, but they aren't our Savior.

Why This Matters to You

1. You Are Never Truly Alone When you are lying in bed at night feeling scared or lonely, remember that the room isn't empty. God's "mighty ones" are stationed around you. You have a massive, invisible support system that is more powerful than any bully, any problem, or any fear you face.

2. There Is More to Your Story Than What You See Your life isn't just about grades, social media, and what you're going to do for a job. You are part of a cosmic drama. Your choices matter in the spiritual realm. When you resist temptation or pray for a friend, there is "joy in the presence of the angels of God" (Luke 15:10). You are part of a Kingdom that spans dimensions.

3. You Don't Have to Fear Evil If you've seen horror movies about demons or ghosts, it's easy to get freaked out. But for a Christian, those things have no power over you. You belong to the King of the spiritual world. "He who is in you is greater than he who is in the world" (1 John 4:4). You are on the winning side.

4. It Inspires Awe of God If the servants (angels) are this incredible, how much more incredible must the Master be? If an archangel bows his face to the ground in the presence of God , it should give us a sense of how holy and amazing our Father really is.

**"For he will command his angels concerning you to guard
you in all your ways;" -** *Psalm 91:11*

Reflect and Talk

1. Why do you think God chose to create an "invisible" world of angels instead of just doing everything Himself?

2. Does knowing that angels are "warriors" rather than "babies with wings" change how you feel about their protection in your life?

3. How does the reality of "Spiritual Warfare" change the way you look at the temptations or negative thoughts you have during the week?

4. If you could see the spiritual world for five minutes, what do you think would surprise you the most about your school or your home?

CHAPTER 19

WHEN JESUS RETURNS

Imagine you are watching a movie that is intense, heartbreaking, and full of suspense. The hero has been beaten down, the villains seem to be winning, and the world is in chaos. If the movie just ended there, you would leave the theater frustrated and confused. You stay in your seat because you know there is a final act. You are waiting for the moment the hero returns, sets things right, and brings peace to the story.

History is God's story, and right now, we are living in the "middle" of the book. It's a time of beauty, but also a time of great pain, sickness, and injustice. However, the Bible promises that the story does not end in a graveyard or a pile of ashes. It ends with the most spectacular event in the history of the universe: the physical, visible, and glorious return of Jesus Christ.

The Promise of the Return

When Jesus ascended into heaven forty days after His resurrection, His disciples stood staring into the sky, probably feeling a mix of awe and abandonment. Suddenly, two angels appeared: *"Men of Galilee,"* they said, *"why do you stand here looking into the sky? This same Jesus, who has been taken from you into heaven, will come back in the same way you have seen him go into heaven."* (Acts 1:11)

This wasn't a new idea. Jesus talked about His return constantly. He told His friends He was going away to "prepare a place" for them and that He would come back to get them. Throughout the New Testament, the writers mention the return of Christ over 300 times. It is the "Blessed Hope" of every Christian.

How Will He Return?

There are many different theories about the specific timeline of the "End Times" (often called **Eschatology**), but almost all Christians agree on these four facts about His coming:

1. **It will be Personal:** It won't be a "spirit" or an "influence." The same Jesus who ate fish with the disciples and has scars in His hands is the one who is coming back.

2. **It will be Visible:** It won't be a secret. Jesus said His coming would be like lightning that flashes from one end of the sky to the other. Everyone will know.

3. **It will be Sudden:** It will happen when people aren't expecting it. Jesus compared it to a "thief in the night."

4. **It will be Glorious:** The first time Jesus came, He came in a quiet stable as a weak baby. The second time He comes, He comes as the King of Kings on a white horse, surrounded by the armies of heaven.

What Will Happen When He Arrives?

The return of Jesus isn't just a grand entrance; it is the moment of ultimate "Restoration." Several massive events will take place:

1. The Resurrection of the Dead

This is one of the most incredible promises in the Bible. When Jesus returns, those who have died "in Christ" will be raised from the dead. They won't be ghosts; they will have new, physical, glorified bodies, bodies that never get sick, never age, and never die. Then, those Christians who are still alive will be transformed in an instant.

2. The Final Judgment

Jesus will settle all accounts. Every secret will be revealed, and every injustice will be addressed. For those who belong to Jesus, this isn't a day of terror, but a day of vindication. Our "Not Guilty" verdict (Justification) will be announced to the whole world. For those who rejected God, it will be the moment they are held accountable for their rebellion.

3. The Defeat of Death and Evil

The Bible says the "last enemy to be destroyed is death" (1 Corinthians 15:26). When Jesus returns, Satan, his demons, and the power of death itself will be thrown into the "lake of fire" forever. They will never be able to hurt, tempt, or destroy God's people again.

4. The New Heavens and the New Earth

God isn't going to scrap the world and start over; He is going to *fix* it. The Bible ends in Revelation 21-22 with a picture of a "New Heaven and a New Earth." It's a place where God lives with His people. There will be no more tears, no more pain, and no more goodbyes.

The "Not Yet" and the "Soon"

A question many people ask is: *If Jesus is coming back to fix everything, why is He waiting so long?*

The Apostle Peter answers this by saying that God isn't slow; He is **patient**. He is holding the door of the Kingdom open as long as possible so that more people have the chance to repent and trust Him (2 Peter 3:9). Every day that Jesus "delays" is another day of mercy for the world.

However, we are called to live in a state of "readiness." We shouldn't be so focused on "predicting" the date that we forget to live for Him today. We live with one eye on our work and one eye on the clouds.

Why This Matters to You

1. It Gives You Perspective on Suffering When you go through a hard time, a breakup, a death in the family, or a struggle with mental health, it can feel like the pain will last forever. The return of Jesus reminds you that "the best is yet to come." Your current suffering is a "chapter," but the ending of the book is joy.

2. It Gives You a Reason to Be Holy If you knew your best friend was coming over to your house in five minutes, you would probably hurry to clean up the mess in your room. Knowing Jesus could return at any moment motivates us to live lives that please Him. We want Him to find us "busy" doing His work when He arrives.

3. It Gives You a Mission If the world is going to be judged and Jesus is the only way to be saved, we have a job to do. We want to bring as many people as possible into the family before the King arrives. It turns our "boring" lives into a rescue mission.

4. It Takes Away the Fear of Death For a Christian, death isn't a "The End" sign; it's a "To Be Continued" sign. We know that even if we die before He returns, we will be raised to live in a world that is more beautiful than anything we can imagine.

"'He will wipe every tear from their eyes. There will be no more death or mourning or crying or pain, for the old order of things has passed away." - *Revelation 21:4*

Reflect and Talk

1. If Jesus returned this afternoon, what is the first thing you would want to say to Him?

2. How does the promise of a "New Earth" (a physical world) change how you think about heaven? (Hint: It's not just sitting on clouds with harps!)

3. Why do you think God wants us to live with the "uncertainty" of when He will return, rather than giving us a specific date?

4. Who is one person in your life you want to tell about Jesus before the story ends?

CHAPTER 20

THE NEW HEAVEN AND THE NEW EARTH

If you have ever reached the final pages of a great epic novel, you know the feeling of "the bittersweet end." You've followed the characters through their darkest moments, cheered for their victories, and mourned their losses. Usually, the story ends with the hero returning home and things going back to "normal."

But the Bible doesn't end with things going back to normal. It doesn't end with us going back to the Garden of Eden. It ends with something far better: a **New Heaven and a New Earth**. This is the final destination of every person who has trusted in Jesus. It is not a place where we sit on clouds playing harps for eternity (which, let's be honest, sounds a bit boring). It is a physical, vibrant, exciting, and perfect world where we finally live life the way it was always meant to be lived.

The Great Restoration: Better Than Before

Many people think that when the world ends, God is going to destroy everything and move us to a distant, ghostly "spirit world." But the Bible uses the word *kainos*, which means "new in quality" or "renewed."

Think of it like a classic car that has been sitting in a junkyard for fifty years. It's rusted, the engine is gone, and the seats are torn. A master restorer doesn't throw the car away; he strips off the rust, replaces the broken parts, and polishes the chrome until it looks better than the day it left the factory.

That is what God is going to do with the universe. He is going to strip away the "rust" of sin, death, and decay. He is going to heal the "cracked foundation" of the earth. The result is a world that is familiar, with mountains, rivers, trees, and cities, but perfected by the presence of God.

In Revelation 21, the Apostle John gets a glimpse of this future world, and he describes it by telling us what *isn't* there. These are often called the "No Mores."

1. No More Sea

In the ancient world, the sea was a symbol of chaos, danger, and separation. When John says there is "no more sea," he isn't saying there won't be water; he's saying there will be no more chaos. The things that threaten us and keep us apart will be gone.

2. No More Death

This is the big one. We live in a world where everything dies, flowers, pets, and the people we love. In the New Earth, death is a defeated enemy. It is an extinct species. You will never have to say goodbye to a loved one ever again.

3. No More Tears or Pain

God Himself is described as leaning down to wipe away every tear from our eyes. This means that the physical pain of sickness and the emotional pain of heartbreak, anxiety, and depression will be completely healed. You won't just "forget" your old sorrows; God will settle them so perfectly that they won't hurt anymore.

4. No More Night

This doesn't mean we won't sleep; it means that the "darkness" of this world, sin, fear, and hidden evil, will have no place there. The glory of God will provide a light that never fades.

The New Jerusalem: The Ultimate City

John sees a vision of a massive city coming down out of heaven called the **New Jerusalem**. This city is the headquarters of the New Earth.

- **The Size:** The city is described as a perfect cube, roughly 1,400 miles long, wide, and high. To put that in perspective, that's about the distance from New York City to the middle of the Rocky Mountains. It is big enough for everyone.

- **The Beauty:** It is made of gold so pure it looks like glass, with walls of jasper and gates made of single pearls. This is the Bible's way of saying that the most valuable things on earth (like gold) will be so common in the New Earth that we'll walk on them like pavement.

- **The Garden-City:** In the middle of the city is the "Tree of Life" and the "River of the Water of Life." This tells us that the New Earth is a perfect blend of nature and culture. It's the best parts of a beautiful forest and the best parts of a vibrant city joined together.

What Will We Actually Do There?

One of the reasons many teens aren't excited about heaven is that they think it will be one long, never-ending church service. But the Bible suggests a much more active future.

1. We Will Work

Wait, work?! Yes, but not the kind of work that makes you tired and stressed. In the beginning, Adam and Eve were given work to do in the Garden, and it was a joy. In the New Earth, we will have projects, creativity, and responsibilities. Maybe you'll compose music, design buildings, or study the stars. You will finally have the time and the perfect brain to do what you were created to do.

2. We Will Rule

The Bible says we will "reign with Him forever and ever" (Revelation 22:5). We will be given authority to manage and care for God's creation. We are the King's children, and we will help Him run the Kingdom.

3. We Will Eat and Drink

Jesus promised that we would eat and drink at His table in the Kingdom. Imagine the best meal you've ever had, shared with the most interesting people in history, without ever feeling full or getting a stomachache. The New Earth is a place of physical pleasure and celebration.

4. We Will See His Face

This is the "Beatific Vision", the greatest reward of all. "They will see his face, and his name will be on their foreheads" (Revelation 22:4). In this life, God feels hidden or distant sometimes. In the New Earth, His presence will be as obvious as the sun. We will talk with Him, walk with Him, and know Him fully.

The "New" Body: Resurrection Life

You won't be a floating ghost in the New Earth. You will have a physical body. When Jesus rose from the dead, He had a "resurrection body." He could be touched, He could eat, and He could be recognized, but He could also travel in ways we don't understand.

- **No More Limitations:** If you have a disability, a chronic illness, or a body that you struggle to like, the New Earth offers a "software and hardware update." You will be you, but the "best" version of you, strong, healthy, and vibrant forever.
- **Recognizing Friends:** You will know your friends and family. The relationships you started on earth will continue and deepen in ways that aren't possible now.

How Do We Get There?

The most important thing about the New Jerusalem is that the gates are never shut, but "nothing impure will ever enter it" (Revelation 21:27).

This brings us back to the very beginning of our journey in this book. How can we, as sinners, enter a perfect world? The answer is only through the **Lamb of God**. Only those whose names are written in the "Lamb's Book of Life" can enter.

Jesus is the "Passover Lamb" who took our sin so that we could be clothed in His righteousness. He is the one who paid the "entry fee" for us. Heaven isn't a place for "good people"; it's a place for **forgiven people**.

Why This Matters to You

1. It Defines Your "True Home" Sometimes you might feel like you don't fit in at school or even in your own family. That's because you were made for a different world. Knowing that the New Earth is coming allows you to be "homesick for a place you've never been." It takes the pressure off this life to be perfect.

2. It Gives Value to the Here and Now If God is going to *renew* the earth rather than destroy it, then what we do now matters. The art you create, the kindness you show, and the way you care for the environment are all "previews" of the coming Kingdom. We are practicing for our forever home.

3. It Provides Absolute Hope No matter how bad your life gets, no matter how much you lose, you have a "guaranteed inheritance" that cannot be stolen or destroyed. The worst thing that can happen to you on this earth (death) is actually the doorway to the best thing that can ever happen to you.

4. It Fuels Your Mission When you realize how beautiful the New Earth is going to be, you won't want anyone to miss out. It gives you the urgency to share the Gospel with your friends. You aren't just trying to "save souls" for a ghost-world; you're inviting them to a literal, physical, eternal party.

> **"He who testifies to these things says, "Yes, I am coming soon." Amen. Come, Lord Jesus". - *Revelation 22:20***

Reflect and Talk

1. If you could do one activity in the New Earth (surfing, playing an instrument, exploring a new planet) for eternity without ever getting tired, what would it be?

2. How does the idea of "No More Tears" help you when you are dealing with a hard situation right now?

3. What do you think it will be like to see Jesus' face for the first time? What is the first question you'll ask Him?

4. How does the reality of a "New Earth" make the Gospel feel more like "Good News" compared to the idea of just "going to heaven" as a ghost?

CONCLUSION

LIVING YOUR FAITH EVERY DAY

You have reached the final pages of this journey. We have traveled from the heights of the character of God to the depths of human brokenness. We have stood at the foot of the cross, peeked into the empty tomb, and looked forward to the renewal of all things in the New Heaven and the New Earth. But as you close this book, a new chapter begins—the one written by your life.

Theology is not just for libraries or classrooms; it is for the kitchen table, the locker room, the social media feed, and the quiet moments of your room. If what you believe doesn't change how you live, then you haven't truly believed it yet. Living your faith every day is the process of taking these massive truths and "putting skin on them." It is about becoming a living, breathing representative of the King in a world that is hungry for hope.

The Integration: Faith is Not a Compartment

Most people in our world live "compartmentalized" lives. They have a "school box," a "friend box," a "family box," and perhaps a "Sunday morning box." They behave differently depending on which box they are in. But the call of Jesus is a call to **integrity**. The word *integrity* comes from the same root as *integer*; it means a whole number, something that cannot be divided.

Living your faith every day means there is no "secular" part of your life. Every square inch of your existence belongs to God. Whether you are studying for a math test, playing a video game, or hanging out at the mall, you are doing it in the presence of God and for the glory of God.

The Daily Rhythm: Morning, Noon, and Night

How do we actually do this? It starts with creating a rhythm. Just as your heart has a beat and your lungs have a breath, your spiritual life needs a cadence.

1. The Morning: The Orientation

Before you check your notifications, before you look at your schedule, you must orient your heart. This is the time to remind yourself of who you are. You are a child of God, adopted by grace, and empowered by the Spirit.

- **The "Yes":** Start the day by saying "Yes" to God's will before you even know what the day holds.

- **The Scripture:** Read even just a few verses to set the "tone" for your mind. Let God's voice be the first one you hear.

2. The Noon: The Alignment

The middle of the day is usually when the "flesh" starts to take over. You're tired, someone was rude to you, or you're stressed about a deadline. This is the time for "breath prayers." A simple, five-second prayer like, *"Lord, give me your patience right now,"* or *"Father, remind me that you are with me,"* can realign your soul in the middle of the chaos.

3. The Night: The Examination

Before you sleep, practice the "Examen." This is an ancient way of looking back at the day with God.

- **Gratitude:** What were the "grace moments" today? Where did you see God working?

- **Confession:** Where did you stumble? Don't hide it; bring it to the light, receive forgiveness, and leave it at the foot of the cross.

- **Trust:** Hand the day back to God. You can sleep because He never does.

Faith in the Classroom: The Mystery of Stewardship

For most of you, "work" is school. You might think that math, history, or science have nothing to do with your faith, but that couldn't be further from the truth.

If God created the world, then every subject you study is an exploration of His handiwork.

- **Science** is the study of how God organized the physical world.

- **Math** is the study of the logic and order God built into the universe.

- **History** is the story of God's providence and human nature.

- **Art and Literature** are expressions of the creativity God placed in us because we are made in His image.

When you work hard in school, you aren't just doing it for a grade or to get into a good college; you are doing it as an act of worship. Excellence is a way of saying "Thank You" to God for the brain He gave you. Integrity in school means not cheating—not because you're afraid of getting caught, but because you know that God sees your heart and values truth more than a GPA.

The Challenge of Secular Education

In many classrooms, God is left out of the conversation. You might feel like you have to check your faith at the door. But a robust theology allows you to engage with secular ideas without being swept away by them. You can learn from the brilliance of secular thinkers while filtering their ideas through the lens of Scripture. When you encounter ideas that contradict God's Word, you don't have to be angry; you can be curious and prayerful, asking the Holy Spirit to help you see where the truth has been twisted.

Faith in the Social Circle: The Ministry of Presence

Your friends are the people who will see your faith most clearly. You don't necessarily have to "preach" at them every day. In fact, sometimes the best witness is simply being a different kind of friend.

1. The Gossip-Stopper

In a world where everyone talks behind everyone's back, a person who refuses to participate in gossip stands out like a neon light. When you choose to speak well of others or simply remain silent when others are being torn down, you are reflecting the heart of a God who is Truth and Love.

2. The Listener

Everyone wants to be heard, but few people truly listen. Because you have a Father who listens to you, you can afford to be the friend who listens to others. Sometimes, "living your faith" just looks like sitting with a friend who is crying and not trying to "fix" them with a clichéd Bible verse, but just being there because Jesus is "with us" in our pain.

3. The Forgiver

Conflict is inevitable. But while the world holds grudges and cancels people, the Christian has a superpower: Forgiveness. When you are the first one to say, "I'm sorry," or the first one to say, "I forgive you," you are putting the Gospel on display. You are showing them what Jesus did for you.

Faith on the Screen: The Digital Frontier

We cannot talk about daily life without talking about your digital life. Your phone is perhaps the place where your faith is most tested.

The Trap of Comparison

Social media is designed to make you feel "less than." It shows you the highlight reels of everyone else's life while you are living your "behind-the-scenes." Living your faith means finding your identity in what God says about you, not in how many likes or views you get. Before you post, ask yourself: *Am I doing this to be noticed, or am I doing this to be helpful?*

The Power of the Tongue (and the Thumb)

The Bible warns us that the tongue can set a whole forest on fire (James 3). Today, that "tongue" is often our keyboard. Before you leave a comment or share a post, ask: *Is this true? Is this kind? Is this necessary?* A Christian's digital footprint should be one of peace, not outrage.

The Hard Days: When Faith Feels Dry

There will be days, sometimes weeks or months, where you don't "feel" God. You'll read your Bible and it will feel like reading a phone book. You'll pray and it will feel like the words are hitting the ceiling.

This is normal. Faith is not a feeling; it is a commitment. Just as a pilot flies by the instruments when they can't see through the clouds, we live by the "instruments" of God's Word when we can't see His hand.

- **Keep Showing Up:** Don't stop praying just because you don't feel "goosebumps."

- **Lean on the Family:** This is why you need the church. When your faith is weak, you can lean on the faith of others.

- **Look Back:** Remind yourself of what God has done in the past. If He was faithful then, He is faithful now, even in the "dark."

The Dark Night of the Soul

Theologians sometimes call these periods of dryness the "dark night of the soul." It isn't necessarily a sign of sin; it's often a sign of growth. God is teaching you to love Him for who He is, not just for the "spiritual high" He gives you. When you keep choosing God even when it feels hard, your faith is being refined into something much stronger and more beautiful than a mere feeling.

Developing a Christian Worldview

Living your faith every day means developing a "Christian Worldview." This is the lens through which you see everything. A worldview answers the four biggest questions of life:

1. **Origin:** Where did I come from? (Creation)

2. **Meaning:** Why am I here? (Imago Dei and Glory)

3. **Morality:** What is wrong with the world? (Fall)

4. **Destiny:** Where is everything going? (Redemption and Restoration)

When you watch a movie, listen to a song, or read a news article, you should be asking: *What is this telling me about these four questions?* If a movie tells you that you are just a collection of chemicals with no purpose, your worldview allows you to say, "I know that's not true because I am made in the image of God." Living your faith means being an active thinker, not a passive consumer.

The Theology of the Mundane

One of the most radical things you can learn as a young Christian is that God cares about the "boring" parts of your day. We often look for God in the "big" moments, the mountain-top retreats, the emotional youth group nights, or the answered miracles. But God is just as present when you are washing the dishes, walking the dog, or sitting in traffic.

The Apostle Paul tells us, *"Whatever you do, work at it with all your heart, as working for the Lord, not for human masters,"* (Colossians 3:23). This means there is no such thing as a "useless" task if it is done for God. When you do your chores with a good attitude, you are serving Christ. When you take care of your body through exercise and rest, you are honoring the temple of the Holy Spirit. This "theology of the mundane" turns your entire life into an ongoing act of worship.

The Stewardship of Time and Talents

God has given you a unique set of gifts, personality traits, and a specific amount of time. Living your faith means being a good "steward" of these resources. Stewardship isn't just about money; it's about managing everything God has put in your hands.

Identifying Your Gifts

You might be good at art, or sports, or explaining complex things, or making people laugh. These aren't just "talents"; they are gifts from the Spirit meant to be used for the good of others. Ask yourself: *How can I use my skill in [blank] to bless someone else this week?*

Prioritizing Your Time

Time is the most limited resource you have. In a world full of distractions, living your faith means being intentional. It doesn't mean you can never watch Netflix or play games, but it means those things shouldn't be the center of your world. It means making time for the things that last forever: your relationship with God and your relationships with people.

The Battle for the Mind: Mental Health and Faith

We live in a time where many young people struggle with anxiety, depression, and mental health challenges. Living your faith does not mean you "shouldn't" struggle with these things. Faith is not a magic shield that makes life easy.

However, theology gives us a place to stand when our minds feel like they are betraying us.

- **The Truth of Your Worth:** When your brain tells you that you are worthless, the Gospel tells you that you were worth the life of the Son of God.

- **The Comfort of the Comforter:** The Holy Spirit is called the Comforter for a reason. He is with you in the panic and the darkness.

- **The Grace for Medicine and Therapy:** God has provided wisdom through doctors and therapists. Seeking help is not a lack of faith; it is a stewardship of the brain God gave you.

Living your faith in the midst of mental health struggles means being honest about your pain while clinging to the hope that your "feelings" aren't the ultimate truth—God's Word is.

Living as a Resurrected Person

Living your faith every day means living as a "resurrected person." This means you no longer have to live as a slave to your old habits.

If you struggled with a quick temper, you aren't "just an angry person" anymore. You are a new creation. You have the power of the Spirit to choose a different path. This doesn't happen all at once (that's Sanctification), but it starts with a change in identity. You don't "try" to be good to get God's love; you "act" like who you already are, a beloved child of the King.

The Great Commission: Your Role in the Big Story

As we conclude, remember that your life is not just about your own personal growth. You have been drafted into a mission. Before Jesus left, He gave us the **Great Commission**: *"Therefore go and make disciples of all nations, baptizing them in the name of the Father and of the Son and of the Holy Spirit,"* (Matthew 28:19).

This sounds intimidating, but it starts in your daily life.

- **Identify:** Who has God placed in your life who doesn't know Him? Your lab partner? Your teammate? Your sibling?

- **Invest:** How can you serve them and love them? Sometimes the best way to share the Gospel is to be the only person who actually cares about their life.

- **Invite:** When the time is right, can you tell them the story of the King who rescued you? You don't need all the answers; you just need to share what you've seen and heard.

You are an ambassador. Everywhere you go, from the coffee shop to the classroom, you are representing a different Kingdom. You are a scout for the New Earth, showing people a "preview" of what is to come through your joy, your hope, and your love.

The Final Charge: Stay the Course

Theology is meant to lead to doxology (praise). All this knowledge about God should make you love Him more. This book was never intended to just fill your head with facts; it was intended to set your heart on fire.

Don't be afraid of the journey ahead. You have the Word of God as your map, the Holy Spirit as your power, and the Church as your traveling companions. And most importantly, you have a Savior who has promised: *"and teaching them to obey everything I have commanded you. And surely I am with you always, to the very end of the age."* (Matthew 28:20).

There will be moments when you want to give up. There will be seasons where the world seems too loud and God seems too quiet. In those moments, remember the empty tomb. Remember that the same power that conquered death is currently at work in you.

Go out into the world. Be bold in your convictions. Be humble in your interactions. Be kind to the broken. Live like someone who has been rescued, because you have. Live like someone who is going to live forever, because you are.

A Final Prayer for the Reader

Heavenly Father,

I thank you for the person reading these words right now. I thank you that they are not an accident, but a masterpiece created by You for a specific purpose in this generation. You knew them before the foundation of the world, and You have called them by name.

Lord, I pray that the truths in this book would move from their head to their heart, and from their heart to their hands. May they not just be "hearers" of the Word, but "doers." When they feel weak, remind them of Your strength. When they feel lonely, remind them of Your presence. When they feel like a failure, remind them of Your grace which is new every morning.

Give them the courage to stand for truth in a world that often calls evil good and good evil. Give them the compassion to love the unlovable and to see people as You see them. Help them to see their school, their home, and their future through the lens of Your Kingdom.

May their life be a "thank you" note to You for all You have done. May they grow in the knowledge of Jesus Christ and bear fruit that lasts. We look forward with joy to the day we see You face to face and hear the words, "Well done, good and faithful servant."

Until then, help us to run the race with endurance, looking to Jesus, the founder and perfecter of our faith.

In the name of Jesus, the King of Kings and Lord of Lords, Amen.

PART 2: SYSTEMATIC THEOLOGY WORKBOOK FOR TEENS

Guided Questions and Real-Life Application for Christian Living

INTRODUCTION

START RIGHT HERE

Read and Learn: Why Truth Matters for Your Life Today

You probably have a lot of voices in your ear every day. Your phone buzzes with news and trends. Your friends at school talk about what is right and what is wrong. Your teachers give you facts and theories. Even the music you listen to tells a story about how you should live. All these voices try to tell you what is true. Some people say that truth changes. They say you can have "your truth" and they can have theirs. This makes life feel like you are walking on shifting sand. If everything is true, then nothing is really true. This leaves you feeling lost when life gets hard.

You need a solid place to stand. You need to know what is real and what lasts forever. This is where theology comes in. The word "theology" sounds big and heavy. It sounds like something for old men in dusty libraries. But the word is actually quite simple. It comes from two Greek words: *Theos*, which means God, and *logos*, which means word or study. So, theology is just the study of God. Systematic theology is even

119

simpler. It means we put those truths in order. We look at what the whole Bible says about one topic at a time. We put the pieces of the puzzle together so we can see the big picture.

You are already a theologian. Every time you think about God, you are doing theology. When you wonder why bad things happen, you are doing theology. When you pray for help before a test, you are doing theology. The question is not whether you are a theologian. The question is whether your theology is good or bad. Is it based on your feelings? Is it based on what a famous person said on the internet? Or is it based on what God has actually told us?

Knowing the truth about God changes how you see yourself. It changes how you treat your parents. It changes how you spend your time on a Friday night. God is the creator of everything. He made the stars, the oceans, and your very heart. He is the source of all truth. If we want to know how life works, we have to look at Him. We cannot just guess about God. We cannot make Him up in our own image. We have to see Him as He really is.

Many teens feel like the Bible is just a list of rules. They think God is a judge who waits for them to mess up. But systematic theology shows us a different story. It shows us a God who is holy, yes, but also a God who is full of love. It shows us that God has a plan for history and a plan for you. When you learn these truths, they act like a compass. They point you in the right direction when you feel confused. They give you a reason to hope when things look dark.

This book is a tool for your life. It is not just a textbook for a grade. Each page helps you build a foundation. You will look at what the Bible says about the Word of God, about Jesus, and about the future. You will see how these ideas fit together. Truth is not a cage. It is a key. It sets you free to live the way God meant for you to live.

Why do we need to do this now? Why not wait until you are older? The world wants your mind right now. Advertisements want your money. Apps want your attention. If you do not know what you believe, you will follow whoever speaks the loudest. You will be like a boat without an anchor. A strong faith starts with strong truth. When you know who God is, you can stand firm. You can say "no" to things that hurt you and "yes" to things that bring life.

Think of this workbook as a map. A map does not just tell you where things are. It tells you how to get where you want to go. You want a life that matters. You want a life that feels right and good. That kind of life only comes when you walk with God. To walk with Him, you must know Him. This book will help you do that. We will keep things clear. We will keep things direct. We will focus on the Bible.

Are you ready to build something that lasts? Truth is waiting for you. Let's look at what God has said. Let's see how His words change your world today. This is the start of a new way to see everything.

Apply and Act: Check Your Beliefs and Set Your Goals

This part of the chapter is for you to work through. Grab a pen. Be honest with yourself. There are no wrong answers here, only chances to grow.

1. The Truth Audit

Think about the things you believe right now. Where did those ideas come from? Fill out the table below to see who is influencing your thoughts about God and life.

Topic	What do I believe about this?	Where did I learn this?
Who is God?		
Why am I here?		
What is sin?		
What happens after death?		

Is the Bible true?		

2. The Anchor Test

When you have a bad day or a big problem, what do you do first? Do you check your phone? Do you talk to a friend? Do you pray? Write down your "first response" to stress.

My First Response:____

____

Now, ask yourself: Does this response help me find the truth, or does it just help me forget the problem?

3. Setting Your Goals

You are starting a study that covers the main parts of Christian belief. What do you want to get out of this? Pick three goals from the list below or write your own.

- [   ] I want to know why I can trust the Bible.
- [   ] I want to be able to explain my faith to my friends.
- [   ] I want to feel closer to God when I pray.
- [   ] I want to stop feeling confused about what is right and wrong.
- [   ] I want to see how the Bible fits together.
- [   ] Other:

____

____

4. Real-Life Application: The "Social Media" Challenge

Scroll through your favorite social media app for five minutes. Look at the posts, the ads, and the comments.

- List three "truths" the app is trying to tell you (Example: "You need this product to be happy" or "You are not pretty enough").

____

____

Next to each one, write one word that describes how that "truth" makes you feel (Example: anxious, jealous, excited).

- Compare these "truths" to what you know about God. Does God say you need that product to be happy? Does He say your worth is based on your looks?

5. Guided Reflection Questions

Answer these questions in one or two sentences. Keep it brief and clear.

- If someone asked you "Who is God?" right now, what would you say?

- What is the biggest question you have about the Bible?

- Why do you think it is important for a teen to study theology in 2026?

----

6. A Simple Prayer to Start

Theology is not just a head exercise. It is a heart matter. Read this prayer out loud as you start this book:

"Lord, I want to know You as You really are. Please clear my mind of lies. Help me to see the truth in Your Word. Give me the strength to change my life based on what I learn. I give this time to You. Amen."

7. Commitment Check

To get the most value from this workbook, you need to be consistent.

- **When** will you work on this each week? (Example: Tuesday nights at 7:00 PM)

- **Where** will you sit so you don't get distracted?

- **Who** can you talk to about what you are learning? (A parent, a youth leader, or a friend)

CHAPTER 1

STUDY THE WORD (BIBLIOLOGY)

Read and Learn: How God Speaks to Us Through the Bible

If you want to know a person, you have to listen to them talk. You cannot just guess what your best friend thinks about a movie. You have to ask them. You cannot assume your coach is happy with your performance. You have to hear their feedback. The same is true with God. We cannot just look at the clouds and guess what God wants from us. We cannot look at a sunset and know how to get to heaven. Those things show us that God is big and strong. But they do not tell us His name. They do not tell us His plan. For that, we need His words.

Theology starts with a big idea: God spoke. He did not leave us in the dark. He chose to tell us who He is. We call this "revelation." It simply means that God pulled back the curtain. He showed us things we could never find on our own. The main way He does this is through the Bible. This is why we start our study here. If we cannot trust the Bible, we cannot trust anything else we learn about God. The Bible is the foundation for every other truth in this book.

You might hear people say the Bible is just a collection of old stories. They might say it was written by men who lived in tents thousands of years ago. In one way, they are right. Men did write the words down. But there is more to the story. The Bible tells us that "all Scripture is breathed out by God." This comes from 2 Timothy 3:16. Think about that for a second. When you speak, you use your breath. God "breathed" His truth into the minds of the writers. We call this "inspiration."

Inspiration does not mean the writers were like robots. God did not take over their hands and force them to write. Instead, He used their personalities. He used their life experiences. Peter sounds like a fisherman because he was one. Paul sounds like a lawyer because he was trained like one. Yet, every word they wrote was exactly what God wanted said. This is a miracle. It means the Bible is 100% the work of men and 100% the work of God.

Because God is the true author, the Bible has a special quality. It is "inerrant." This is a fancy way of saying it does not have any errors. God does not lie. God does not make mistakes. If the Bible is God's Word, then the Bible must be true in everything it says. It is true when it talks about history. It is true when it talks about science. Most importantly, it is true when it talks about how you can be saved. You can trust it more than you trust your own feelings. Feelings change every day. The Word of God stays the same.

The Bible is also "sufficient." This means it gives us everything we need to know God and follow Him. You do not need a secret code to find God. You do not need a new vision or a special dream. God has already said what He needs to say in the 66 books of the Bible. It is a complete map for your life. It tells you where you came from. It tells you why the world is broken. It tells you how Jesus fixes that brokenness.

Lastly, the Bible has "authority." Since God is the King of the universe, His words are the final law. When the Bible says something is wrong, it is wrong. When it says something is good, it is good. We do not get to pick and choose the parts we like. We do not get to cut out the verses that

126

make us feel uncomfortable. Following the Bible means we put God in the driver's seat. We let Him set the rules for our relationships, our money, and our time.

Reading the Bible is not just about gaining facts. It is about meeting a Person. When you open your Bible, you are sitting down to listen to the Creator of the stars. He wants to talk to you. He wants to guide you. But you have to show up. You have to read. You have to listen. This chapter will help you see how to do that well. It will show you how the Bible is organized. It will help you see why it is the most important book you will ever own.

The world will tell you that the Bible is outdated. People will say it does not fit with modern life. Do not believe them. The grass withers and the flowers fall, but the Word of our God stands forever. This is the only book that can truly change your heart. It is the only book that offers real hope. Let's look at how we can study it and live it out.

Apply and Act: Use a Study Plan and Verify Bible Facts

This section is your chance to put what you just read into practice. Use these exercises to build your confidence in the Word of God.

1. The Structure of the Book

The Bible is one big story, but it is made of many smaller parts. Test your knowledge by filling in the blanks below.

- The Bible has _________ total books.
- There are ________ books in the Old Testament.
- There are ________ books in the New Testament.
- The Bible was written by about ________ different authors.
- It was written over a period of about ________ years.

2. Inspiration vs. Human Ideas

Read 2 Peter 1:20-21. In your own words, explain how a human author wrote a book that actually came from God.

____

____

____

____

3. The "Inerrancy" Case Study

Imagine a friend at school says, "The Bible was written by people, and people make mistakes. So, the Bible must have mistakes too." Based on what you learned in the "Read and Learn" section, how would you answer them? (Hint: Think about who was guiding the authors).

---

4. Bible Fact Check

Pick one of the following verses. Look it up in your Bible and answer the questions below.

Options: Psalm 119:105, Hebrews 4:12, or John 17:17.

- **Verse Reference:**

- **What does this verse say about the Word of God?**

- **How can you apply this verse to a problem you are facing today?**

---

5. Practice the "COMA" Method

When you read the Bible, it helps to have a system. Use the **COMA** method on **John 1:1-5**.

- **C - Context:** Who wrote this? Who was it written to? (A quick look at the intro to John in your Bible can help).

- **O - Observation:** What is happening in these verses? What words are repeated?

- **M - Meaning:** What is the main point the author is trying to make about Jesus (the Word)?

- **A - Application:** How does knowing that Jesus is "the Word" change how you think about God?

  ----

6. Real-Life Application: The Authority Test

Think about a popular opinion in our culture today (Example: "You should always do what makes you happy").

- **The Opinion:**

- **What does the Bible say about this?** (Look for a verse about following God's will instead of our own).

- **Which authority will you follow? Why?**

  ----

7. A 7-Day Bible Reading Plan

Commit to reading the Word every day for one week. Use the checklist below. Read the passage and write one thing you learned about God from it.

Day	Passage	What I Learned About God
Day 1	Psalm 19	
Day 2	Psalm 119:1-16	
Day 3	2 Timothy 3:10-17	
Day 4	Matthew 4:1-11	
Day 5	Isaiah 40:1-8	
Day 6	Deuteronomy 6:1-9	
Day 7	Revelation 22:18-21	

8. Clear Obstacles

What is the biggest thing that stops you from reading the Bible? Is it being busy? Is it being bored? Is it not knowing where to start?

\---

\---

Write down one specific change you can make this week to overcome that obstacle. (Example: "I will put my phone in another room while I read for ten minutes.")

\---

\---

9. Summary Question

If the Bible is God's personal message to you, how should that change the way you look at the book on your nightstand?

\---

\---

10. Memory Verse Challenge

Try to memorize **Psalm 119:11** this week: *"I have stored up your word in my heart, that I might not sin against you."* Write the verse here three times to help it stick in your mind:

1. ____

2. ____

3. ____

CHAPTER 2

PRAISE THE FATHER (THEOLOGY PROPER)

Read and Learn: Who God Is and Why He Created You

When you hear the word "God," what comes to your mind? Maybe you think of a bright light in the sky. Maybe you think of a strict judge in a courtroom. Or maybe you think of a kind old man sitting on a cloud. Most people have an image of God, but often that image is wrong. We tend to make God look like us. We think He gets moody or tired or surprised. But God is nothing like a human. He is the Creator, and we are the creation. In this chapter, we look at "Theology Proper." This is just a way of saying we are studying God Himself.

To know God, we have to look at His traits. We call these "attributes." These are the things that are always true about Him. Some of these traits belong to God alone. For example, God is "infinite." This means He has

132

no limits. He has no beginning and no end. He does not need sleep. He never runs out of energy. He does not need anyone to help Him. Before the stars existed, God was there. After the earth is gone, God will still be there. This makes Him different from everything else in the universe. Everything we see has a limit, but God is limitless.

Another trait is that God is "immutable." This means He never changes. Think about how much you change. You grow taller. Your tastes in music change. Your moods go up and down. But God is the same yesterday, today, and forever. His promises do not expire. His love does not fade. His rules do not shift based on what is popular. This is good news. It means you can count on Him. When the world feels like it is spinning out of control, God is the rock that never moves.

God is also "omniscient." This means He knows everything. He knows the number of hairs on your head. He knows what you are going to say before you speak. He knows your secrets and your dreams. You can never hide from Him, but you also never have to explain yourself to Him. He already understands. Along with this, He is "omnipotent," or all-powerful. He created the world with a word. He rules over kings and nations. There is no problem in your life that is too big for Him to handle. Finally, He is "omnipresent." He is everywhere at the same time. You are never alone. Whether you are at school, at home, or in a foreign country, God is right there with you.

These traits show us how big God is. But God is not just a powerful force. He is a Person. The Bible tells us that God is "holy." This means He is perfect. He has no sin. He is completely set apart from evil. Because He is holy, He is also "just." He must punish wrong things. He cannot just look the other way when people get hurt. But the Bible also says that "God is love." His love is not a feeling that comes and goes. It is who He is. He is patient. He is kind. He is merciful. He wants a relationship with you.

The most amazing thing about God is that He is our Father. Jesus told us to pray to "Our Father in heaven." This changes everything. It means the Creator of the galaxy wants you to call Him "Abba." This is a word that shows closeness and trust. A good father protects his children. He provides for them. He listens to them. God is the perfect version of a father. Even if your earthly father is not around or has let you down, your Heavenly Father never will.

Why did this great God create you? He did not create you because He was lonely. He was already happy within Himself. He created you to show off His glory. He made you so you could know Him and enjoy Him forever. When you live for God, you are doing what you were made to do. You are like a lightbulb that has finally been plugged in. You start to shine.

Knowing who God is should lead us to worship. When we see how big He is, we feel small in a good way. We realize that we do not have to carry the weight of the world. God has it. We can stop trying to be in control and let Him lead. We can trade our worry for praise. This week, we will focus on seeing God for who He really is. We will move past our small ideas and look at the Great King.

Apply and Act: Map Out God's Traits and See Them in the World

This workbook section helps you move from knowing facts about God to trusting Him in real life.

1. The Attribute Map

In the boxes below, write down four of God's attributes that you just learned about. Under each one, write one way that specific trait helps you today.

Attribute	How this helps me today
Example: Immutable	*I don't have to worry if God is mad at me today, because His love stays the same.*
1.	
2.	
3.	

<table>
<tr><td>4.</td><td></td></tr>
</table>

2. Word Study: Holy

Read **Isaiah 6:1-5**.

- How did Isaiah feel when he saw the holiness of God?

- Why do you think we sometimes forget that God is holy and perfect?

  ----

3. Case Study: The Midnight Worry

Imagine you are lying in bed at midnight. You are worried about a big test tomorrow. You feel like you are all alone and that nobody understands your stress.

- Which attribute of God (Omniscience, Omnipotence, or Omnipresence) applies to this situation?

- Write a one-sentence prayer using that attribute to calm your heart.

  ----

4. The Creation Scavenger Hunt

God's power and beauty are visible in the world He made. Spend 10 minutes outside or looking out a window. Find three things that show you something about God's character.

- **Thing 1:**____
  What it shows about God: _______________________________
- **Thing 2:** ____
  What it shows about God: _______________________________
- **Thing 3:** ____
  What it shows about God: _______________________________

5. "Abba" Reflection

Read **Matthew 7:9-11**. Jesus compares God to an earthly father.

- If God is a "good Father" who gives "good gifts," how should that change the way you ask Him for things in prayer?

----

6. Sorting Truth from Lies

Check the boxes next to the statements that are Biblically true about God.

- [   ] God is sometimes surprised by the news.
- [   ] God has always existed.
- [   ] God's love for you depends on how good you are today.
- [   ] God is present even when you feel lonely.
- [   ] God is the same today as He was in the Old Testament.

7. Real-Life Application: The Glory Challenge

We were made to reflect God's glory. This means we should act in a way that makes God look good to others.

- Pick one attribute of God you can reflect this week (Example: God is merciful, so I will be merciful to my sibling).

  My Attribute:

The Plan: What is one specific action you will take to show this trait to someone else?

----

8. Guided Reflection Questions

Answer these briefly:

- If God knows everything you do (Omniscience), does that make you feel scared or safe? Why?

- Which attribute of God is the hardest for you to understand?

- How does knowing God is "Immutable" (unchanging) help you when your friends or family change?

  ----

9. The Praise List

Take two minutes to write down as many names or descriptions of God as you can think of (Example: King, Shepherd, Rock, Light).

  ----

10. Memory Verse Challenge

Memorize **Psalm 102:27**: *"But you are the same, and your years have no end."* Write it out here and underline the word that describes God's immutability:

  ----

11. A Step Toward Trust

What is one thing in your life right now that feels "out of control"?

Write down which of God's attributes gives you peace about this situation.

CHAPTER 3

WORSHIP THE TRINITY (THE TRINITY)

Read and Learn: How God Lives as Father, Son, and Spirit

The most famous math problem in the Bible is this: $1 + 1 + 1 = 1$. This does not make sense in a school classroom, but it is the truth about who God is. We call this the Trinity. The word "Trinity" is not actually in the Bible, but the idea is on almost every page. It describes a God who is one in essence but three in person. This is the hardest thing for our human brains to grasp. But that is actually a good sign. If we could explain every single thing about God, He would not be much of a God. He is far bigger than our logic.

To start, we must be clear that there is only one God. The Bible is very firm on this. In the Old Testament, the people of Israel said a prayer called the *Shema* every day. It says, "Hear, O Israel: The Lord our God, the Lord is one." Christians do not believe in three gods. We do not have a "main" god and two "helper" gods. We believe in one God. This one God has existed forever as three distinct Persons: the Father, the Son, and the Holy Spirit.

How can one be three? Think about the way God has revealed Himself in the Bible. At the very beginning, in Genesis 1, God says, "Let **us** make man in **our** image." He did not say "Let me make man in my image." There was a conversation happening within God before time began. We see this even more clearly when Jesus is baptized in the Jordan River. The Son is standing in the water. The Holy Spirit descends on Him like a dove. The Father speaks from heaven, saying, "This is my beloved Son." All three Persons are present and active at the same time. They are distinct, but they are not divided.

The three Persons of the Trinity have different roles, but they are all equal in power and glory. The Father is the one who plans and sends. He is the architect of salvation. The Son, Jesus Christ, is the one who obeys the Father and comes to earth. He is the one who died and rose again. The Holy Spirit is the one who applies that work to your life. He lives inside you, teaches you the truth, and gives you strength. They work together in perfect harmony. They never argue. They never have different goals. They are perfectly united in everything they do.

Why does the Trinity matter for your life on a Tuesday afternoon? It matters because God is love. For God to be love before He created humans, He had to have someone to love. Because God is a Trinity, the Father has loved the Son through the Spirit for all eternity. Love is part of who God is, not just something He does. This means that when God loves you, He is inviting you into the same kind of perfect relationship that He has within Himself.

Understanding the Trinity also changes how we pray. We do not just toss words into the air. We pray **to** the Father, **through** the Son, and **by the power of** the Holy Spirit. When you feel like you do not have the right words, the Spirit helps you. When you feel like you are not good enough to talk to God, Jesus stands as your bridge. The Father sits on the throne, ready to listen to His children. The Trinity makes your prayer life possible.

Some people try to explain the Trinity using analogies. They talk about how water can be ice, liquid, or steam. Or they talk about an egg having a shell, a white, and a yolk. These are helpful starts, but they all fall short. Water changes from one form to another, but God never changes. An egg can be broken into parts, but God cannot be divided. It is better to admit that the Trinity is a beautiful mystery. We do not study the Trinity to solve it like a puzzle. We study it so we can worship God for how great He is.

When you think about the Trinity, you should feel a sense of awe. You serve a God who is big enough to create the universe but personal enough to live inside your heart. He is a community within Himself. This shows us that relationships are the most important thing in the world. Since God is a relational Being, you were made for relationship too. You were made to know the Father, love the Son, and walk with the Spirit. This is what it means to be truly alive.

Apply and Act: Find the Trinity in the Bible and in Your Prayers

This section will help you see the Trinity in action and help you think about how this truth changes the way you live.

1. The Trinity Chart

Fill in the chart below to help you remember the distinct roles and the shared nature of the three Persons of God.

Person	His Specific Role	A Verse That Mentions Him
The Father		
The Son		
The Spirit		

2. Scripture Search

Read the following verses and identify which Persons of the Trinity are mentioned in each.

- **Matthew 28:19:**

- **2 Corinthians 13:14:**

- **1 Peter 1:2:**

  ----

3. The "Relationship" Reflection

We learned that God is a "community" of three Persons. Because you are made in His image, you are also meant for community.

- Who are three people in your life that help you grow closer to God?

  1. ____

  2. ____

  3. ____

How can you show the kind of unselfish love that exists between the Father, Son, and Spirit to one of these people today?

  ----

4. Analogy Alert

As we discussed, most analogies for the Trinity (like the egg or the apple) fail in some way.

- Why is it dangerous to think of God as having "three parts" rather than being "three Persons"?

  ----

5. Prayer Practice: The Trinitarian Way

Try writing a short prayer below. Be intentional about how you address each Person of the Trinity.

- **Thank the Father** for a specific blessing:

- **Thank the Son** for what He did on the cross:

- **Ask the Spirit** for help with a specific struggle:

  ----

6. Case Study: The "Three Gods" Question

A friend at school says, "Christians are confusing. You say you believe in one God, but then you talk about Jesus and the Holy Spirit like they are different gods. That's three gods."

- Using what you learned in the "Read and Learn" section, write a 2-sentence response to your friend that is clear and direct.

  ----

7. Real-Life Application: Worship in Focus

Sometimes we focus so much on Jesus that we forget the Father, or we focus on the Spirit and forget Jesus.

- Which Person of the Trinity do you think about or pray to the most?

- Which Person do you think about the least?

- This week, try to find a worship song that focuses on the Person you think about the least. Write the name of the song here:

  ----

8. Guided Reflection Questions

Answer these briefly:

- If God were only one Person, could He have been "Love" before He created the world? Why or why not?

- How does it make you feel to know that the Holy Spirit, who is fully God, lives inside you?

- Does the mystery of the Trinity make you want to study the Bible more or less? Why?

  ----

9. The Great Commission Challenge

Read **Matthew 28:18-20**. This is the last thing Jesus said to His followers.

- Why do you think Jesus told them to baptize new believers "in the name" (singular) of the Father, Son, and Holy Spirit?

  ----

10. Truth vs. Error

Read the statements below and mark them as **Truth** or **Error**.

- The Father created the Son a long time ago. (________)
- The Spirit is just a force, like electricity. (________)
- Jesus is just as much God as the Father is. (________)
- God sometimes acts like the Father and sometimes acts like the Son. (________)

11. Memory Verse Challenge

Memorize **Numbers 6:24-26**, which is an old blessing that reflects the three-fold nature of God's care. Write it out here:

----

12. The Power of Three

Look at your current life goals. How can you involve the Trinity in them?

- **Father (The Plan):** What do you think God's will is for your future?

- **Son (The Way):** How can you follow Jesus' example in your school or work?

- **Spirit (The Power):** Where do you need the Spirit's strength this week?

  ----

13. Final Thought

If God is a perfect community of love, how should that change the way you deal with people you don't like?

CHAPTER 4

VALUE THE PERSON (ANTHROPOLOGY)

Read and Learn: Why Every Human Has Worth and a Purpose

Who are you? If you ask a scientist, they might say you are a collection of cells and atoms. If you ask a coach, they might say you are a midfielder or a point guard. If you ask an app, you are just a set of data points to be sold to advertisers. Most of the messages you hear every day treat you like a product or a biological accident. They suggest that your value comes from what you can do, how you look, or how much money you will make one day. But the Bible tells a completely different story. It tells us that you are a masterpiece designed by the King of the universe.

The study of humans is called "anthropology." In a Bible study context, we look at what God says about His favorite creation. To find your true identity, you have to go back to the very first page of the Bible. In Genesis 1:26, God says, "Let us make man in our image, after our likeness." This is a huge statement. God did not say this about the mountains. He did not say this about the lions or the stars. He only said it about people. We call this the *Imago Dei*, which is Latin for the "Image of God."

Being made in the image of God does not mean you look like God physically. God is spirit, so He does not have a body like we do. Instead, it means you reflect His character. Just as a mirror reflects your face, you were built to reflect God to the world. You have the ability to create because God is the Creator. You have a sense of right and wrong because God is holy. You can speak and communicate because God is a talking God. You have the capacity for deep relationships because God exists in a perfect relationship as the Trinity.

This image of God gives every single person an incredible amount of worth. It does not matter if a person is old or young. It does not matter if they are rich or poor. It does not matter if they are healthy or sick. Every human being has "dignity." This means they deserve respect simply because they exist. When you see a person on the street who is struggling, you are looking at someone made in God's image. When you look at the person you find most annoying at school, you are looking at someone God carefully crafted. This truth should change how you treat everyone you meet.

God did not just make your spirit; He also made your body. Sometimes Christians act like the body is bad and only the soul is good. But that is not what the Bible teaches. God formed the first man out of the dust of the ground and breathed life into him. He made your eyes to see beauty and your ears to hear music. He made your hands to work and your feet to run. Your body is a gift. It is the temple of the Holy Spirit if you follow Jesus. This means how you treat your body matters. What you eat, how you sleep, and how you use your physical strength are all ways to honor God.

Why are we here? What is our job on this planet? God gave the first humans a "dominion mandate." This is a big phrase that just means we are God's representatives on earth. He put us here to take care of the world. We are meant to build things, grow things, and bring order to the chaos. You are not here just to wait for heaven. You are here to reflect God's light into every corner of the earth. Whether you become a doctor, a plumber, or a teacher, your job is to serve God and love people.

However, we have to be honest about one thing. The image of God in us is currently broken. Think of a mirror that has been dropped on the floor. It is still a mirror. It still reflects light. But the reflection is cracked and distorted. That is what happened when sin entered the world. We still have worth, but we also have a "sin nature." We use our words to hurt instead of heal. We use our creativity to make bad things. We forget our purpose and live for ourselves.

The good news is that God is in the business of fixing the mirror. Through Jesus, God is restoring His image in us. As you grow in your faith, you start to look more like the person you were always meant to be. You start to value people the way God does. You start to see yourself not as a failure or an accident, but as a beloved child of the King.

Do you ever feel like you don't fit in? Do you worry that you aren't "enough"? Remember that your value is not a score you have to earn. It is a gift you have already received. You were made on purpose, for a purpose. When you grasp this, you can stop trying to impress people. You can start living for the One who made you.

Apply and Act: Build a Healthy View of Yourself Based on God's Word

This section is designed to help you reject the lies of the world and embrace the truth about who God made you to be.

1. The "Image-Bearer" Audit

How do you see the people around you? Think about three people you interact with regularly. Write their names and one way you can see the "Image of God" in them (their creativity, their kindness, their sense of justice, etc.).

Person's Name	Evidence of God's Image
1.	
2.	
3.	

2. Body and Soul Balance

We are both physical and spiritual beings. Look at your habits from the last week.

- What is one thing you did to care for your **soul** (Example: Prayed, read the Bible)?

- What is one thing you did to care for your **body** (Example: Went for a run, got 8 hours of sleep)?

- Why do you think God cares about both of these things?

  ----

3. The Comparison Trap

We often feel bad about ourselves because we compare our "behind-the-scenes" life to everyone else's "highlight reel" on social media.

- List three things you often compare about yourself to others (Example: looks, grades, popularity).

  1. ____

  2. ____

  3. ____

- Now, read **Psalm 139:13-16**. According to these verses, who is responsible for how you were "knit together"?

- How does this verse answer the three comparisons you listed above?

----

4. Word Study: Stewardship

Being a human means being a "steward" or a manager of God's world.

- List three "talents" or "skills" you have (Example: drawing, being a good listener, math).

    1. ____

    2. ____

    3. ____

- How can you use one of these skills to help someone else this week?

----

5. Real-Life Application: The "Respect Challenge"

Think of someone at school or in your community who is often ignored or treated poorly.

- Their Initials: ________

- **The Plan:** What is one small, respectful action you can take toward them this week to acknowledge their dignity as an image-bearer? (Example: Saying hello by name, sitting with them at lunch).

----

6. Guided Reflection Questions

Answer these in one or two clear sentences.

- If you truly believed that every person you met was made in the image of God, how would your social media comments change?

- Why is it important to know that you are a "broken" image-bearer and not a "perfect" one?

- What is the difference between "self-esteem" (feeling good about yourself) and "God-given worth"?

  ----

7. True or False?

Circle the correct answer based on what you have learned.

- **T / F:** Your value increases when you get better grades.
- **T / F:** Humans are the only part of creation made in God's image.
- **T / F:** The body is a "container" for the soul and does not really matter to God.
- **T / F:** Sin has completely destroyed the image of God in humans.
- **T / F:** Part of being human is having a job to do for God.

8. The "Why Am I Here?" Map

Think about your current life as a teen. Where has God placed you?

- **My Family:** One way I can reflect God here:

- **My School:** One way I can reflect God here:

- **My Friends:** One way I can reflect God here:

  ----

9. Identifying the Lies

What is the most common lie you tell yourself about your worth? (Example: "I am only valuable if I am successful.")

Find a Bible verse that contradicts that lie. (Hint: Use an index or search tool for words like "love," "worth," or "created").

Verse:

----

10. Memory Verse Challenge

Memorize **Genesis 1:27**: *"So God created man in his own image, in the image of God he created him; male and female he created them."* Write it out here from memory:

----

11. Final Action Step

Before you go to bed tonight, look in the mirror and say out loud: "I am made in the image of God, and I have a purpose."

- How does saying that make you feel?

----

12. A Prayer for Identity

"Father, thank You for making me. Thank You that I am not an accident. Help me to see the worth You have given me. Help me to see the worth in every person I meet today. Show me how to use my body and my mind to bring You glory. Amen."

CHAPTER 5

TURN FROM SIN (HAMARTIOLOGY)

Read and Learn: How Sin Breaks Things and Why We Need a Cure

The word "sin" is not very popular today. People prefer to use words like "mistake," "error," or "bad choice." These words make it sound like we just slipped up or tripped. But the Bible uses much stronger language. To understand why the world is a mess and why our own hearts feel restless, we have to look at the root of the problem. In theology, we call the study of sin "Hamartiology." This comes from the Greek word *hamartia*, which means "to miss the mark."

Imagine an archer aiming at a target. The goal is to hit the bullseye. If the arrow flies off to the side or falls short, the archer has missed the mark. God's "mark" for us is perfection. He created us to reflect His character and live in perfect harmony with Him. When we sin, we don't just "mess up." We fail to hit the target of God's holy standard. We fall short of His glory.

Where did this start? It began in a garden. In Genesis 3, we see the first humans, Adam and Eve, make a choice. God gave them everything they needed. He gave them one simple rule: do not eat from the tree of the knowledge of good and evil. But they chose to listen to a lie instead of the truth. They wanted to be like God. They wanted to set their own rules. This was the first act of rebellion. Since Adam was the head of the human race, his choice affected all of us. We are born with a "sin nature." This means we are not just sinners because we sin; we sin because we are sinners. It is part of our DNA from birth.

Sin shows up in two ways. First, there are "sins of commission." these are the bad things we do. It is the lie we tell to stay out of trouble. It is the mean comment we post online. It is the pride we feel when we think we are better than someone else. Second, there are "sins of omission." These are the good things we fail to do. It is when we see someone being bullied and say nothing. It is when we have the chance to help a neighbor but choose to play video games instead. Both types of sin are a rebellion against God.

Theology teaches us about "total depravity." This sounds like a scary phrase, but it is a simple idea. It does not mean that every person is as bad as they could possibly be. It means that every part of a person is touched by sin. Our minds think selfish thoughts. Our hearts love the wrong things. Our bodies are used for selfish goals. Even our "good" deeds are often done for the wrong reasons, like wanting praise from others. Sin is like a drop of ink in a glass of water. It spreads through the whole thing.

Why is sin such a big deal? It is a big deal because of who God is. Because God is perfectly holy, He cannot live in the presence of sin. Sin creates a huge gap between us and our Creator. It is like a wall that we cannot climb. The Bible says the "wages of sin is death." A wage is something you earn for your work. Because of our rebellion, we have earned a spiritual death. This means separation from God now and forever.

Sin also breaks our relationships with other people. When we are selfish, we hurt our friends. When we are dishonest, we break trust with our parents. Every war, every theft, and every broken heart in history can be traced back to sin. It is the great destroyer of peace. It makes us look at others as tools to get what we want instead of people made in God's image.

However, we cannot fix this on our own. You cannot "work off" your sin. You cannot be "good enough" to make up for the bad. If you are drowning in the middle of the ocean, you don't need a swimming lesson; you need a rescue. The law of God is like a mirror. It shows you that your face is dirty, but it cannot wash you. It shows you that you have missed the mark.

Recognizing our sin is the first step toward joy. If you don't know you are sick, you will never go to a doctor. If you don't know you are lost, you will never look at a map. When we admit that we have a sin problem, we are ready for the cure. God does not talk about sin to make us feel worthless. He talks about sin so we can see how much we need Jesus. The bad news of our sin makes the good news of the Savior even better.

This week, don't hide your struggles. Don't pretend you are perfect. Bring your mistakes into the light. When we face the truth about our sin, we find the path to real freedom.

Apply and Act: Track Your Habits and Ask for God's Help to Change

Use this section to look at your own life with honesty. Remember, God already knows your heart. He is ready to forgive and help you grow.

1. Missing the Mark

Think about the last 24 hours.

- List one "sin of commission" (something bad you did):

  ____

  ____

  ____

- List one "sin of omission" (something good you failed to do):

  ____

  ____

  ____

2. The Ripple Effect

Pick one of the sins you listed above. How did it affect other people?

- **Person affected:**

- **The result of the action:**

  ----

3. Scripture Search: The Definition of Sin

Read **1 John 3:4**.

- How does this verse define sin?

- Read **James 4:17**. How does this verse define sin?

  ----

4. The "Total Depravity" Check

How does sin affect these different parts of your life? Give a brief example for each.

- **Your Thoughts:**

- **Your Words:**

- **Your Use of Time:**

  ----

5. Identifying Patterns

Most of us have a "favorite" sin, a struggle that keeps coming back.

- What is one temptation you face almost every day? (Example: Anger, lying, laziness, lust).

- What is usually happening when you face this temptation? (Example: I am tired, I am with certain friends, I am bored on my phone).

  ----

6. The "Mirror" Exercise

Read the **Ten Commandments** in **Exodus 20:1-17**.

- Which commandment is the hardest for you to keep right now?

- Why do you think that specific rule is difficult for you?

  ----

7. Case Study: The "Small" Lie

Imagine you forgot to do your homework. Your teacher asks why it isn't finished. You think about saying your internet was down, even though it wasn't.

- Is this a "small" sin to God? Why or why not?

- What is the "mark" that you would be missing in this situation?

  ----

8. Guided Reflection Questions

Answer these in one or two sentences.

- Why do people often try to rename "sin" as a "mistake"?

- If God is holy, why can't He just ignore our sin?

- How does knowing you have a sin nature help you be more patient with other people's mistakes?

  ----

9. True or False?

- You are only a sinner if you do something really bad like murder.
  (________)
- Sin began with Adam and Eve in the garden.   (________)
- We can fix our sin problem by doing enough good deeds.   (________)
- Sin affects our minds, hearts, and bodies.   (________)
- Every sin is a rebellion against God's authority.   (________)

10. Real-Life Application: The Turning Point

The word for "turning from sin" is **repentance**. It means to change your mind and your direction.

- Pick one habit you want to change this week.

  The Habit:

- **The Turn:** Instead of doing that habit, what is one "holy" thing you can do instead? (Example: Instead of complaining, I will say one thing I am thankful for).

  ----

11. Memory Verse Challenge

Memorize **Romans 3:23**: *"For all have sinned and fall short of the glory of God."* Write it out three times below to help it sink in.

1. ____

2. ____

3. ____

12. The Prayer of Confession

Read **Psalm 51:1-4**. This was King David's prayer after he sinned greatly. Use it as a model to write your own short prayer of confession below.

____

____

____

____

13. Final Thought

If sin is a wall between us and God, who is the only one who can tear that wall down?

____

____

____

____

____

____

____

____

____

____

CHAPTER 6

LOVE THE SAVIOR (CHRISTOLOGY)

Read and Learn: Why Jesus Became a Man to Save His People

If you look at a timeline of human history, everything points to one Person. We even split time into two parts based on His birth. That Person is Jesus Christ. You might know His name from Sunday school or even from people using it as a curse word. But who is He really? In theology, we call this study "Christology." It is the most important topic you will ever study. If you get Jesus wrong, you get God wrong.

The first thing you must know is that Jesus is 100% God. He did not "become" God later in life. He did not just have "godly ideas." He is the eternal Son of God. He was there when the world was created. In fact, the Bible says everything was made through Him. He has all the traits of God that we talked about in Chapter 2. He is all-powerful, all-knowing,

159

and holy. When you look at Jesus, you are looking at God in the flesh.

But here is the miracle: Jesus is also 100% man. This is called the "Incarnation." It means the Creator of the universe took on human skin. He became a baby in a manger. He grew up in a small town. He got hungry. He got tired. He felt physical pain. He even felt the sting of a friend's betrayal. Why did He do this? He did it because a human problem needed a human solution. Since a man (Adam) brought sin into the world, a man had to pay the price for that sin. Jesus had to be human so He could die in our place.

Jesus lived a perfect life. This is a very big deal. You and I "miss the mark" every single day. We fail at the target of holiness. But Jesus never missed once. He was tempted in every way that you are. He felt the pressure to fit in. He felt the pull of anger. But He never sinned. He kept every law of God perfectly. Because He had no sin of His own, He could take the punishment for yours.

Then came the cross. This was not an accident. It was not a tragedy where the "good guy" lost. It was a rescue mission. On the cross, a "divine exchange" happened. Jesus took all your lies, your pride, and your rebellion. He carried them on His shoulders. God treated Jesus as if He had lived your sinful life so that God could treat you as if you had lived Jesus' perfect life. He died the death you deserved to give you the life you could never earn.

If the story ended at the grave, we would still be lost. But three days later, Jesus walked out of the tomb. The resurrection is the proof that God accepted His sacrifice. It proves that Jesus is who He said He is. He beat death. He beat sin. He beat the devil. Today, He is alive. He is sitting at the right hand of God the Father. He is not just a figure from a history book. He is a King who is ruling right now.

Knowing about Jesus is not the same as knowing Him. You can know every stat about a pro athlete and still never meet them. You can know the lyrics to every song by a band and not know the lead singer. Jesus does not want fans; He wants followers. He wants to be the center of your life. He wants to be the one you turn to when you are lonely. He wants to be the one you thank when you are happy.

When you see how much Jesus loved you, it changes how you love others. It takes away your fear of the future. You don't have to prove your worth to anyone because the King of Kings already gave His life for you. You are loved with a love that will never let you go. This week, we will look at His life and see how His steps can guide your own.

Apply and Act: Follow the Steps of Jesus and Learn from His Life

This part of the chapter helps you see Jesus as a real Person who lived a real life. He is not a myth; He is your Savior.

1. The Two Natures of Jesus

We learned that Jesus is both God and Man. Read the verses below and identify which nature (Human or Divine) is being shown.

- **John 11:35** ("Jesus wept"):

- **Mark 4:39** (Jesus calms a storm with a word):

- **John 4:6** (Jesus was tired from his journey):

- **Matthew 9:6** (Jesus forgives sins):

  ----

2. The Life of Christ Timeline

Put these events from the life of Jesus in the correct order (1 to 6).

- [   ] The Resurrection
- [   ] The Baptism in the Jordan River
- [   ] The Birth in Bethlehem
- [   ] The Ascension to Heaven
- [   ] The Temptation in the Wilderness
- [   ] The Death on the Cross

3. Case Study: Temptation at School

Imagine a group of students is making fun of a teacher behind their back. They want you to join in. You feel the pressure to say something mean to fit in.

- Read **Hebrews 4:15**. How does knowing Jesus was tempted "in every way" help you in this moment?

- Since Jesus lived a perfect life, what kind of strength can He give you to say "no" to this group?

  ----

4. Word Study: Propitiation

This is a big word that means "a sacrifice that turns away anger."

- Read **1 John 2:2**. According to this verse, who is the sacrifice for our sins?

- How does it make you feel to know that Jesus took the "anger" or judgment that you earned?

  ----

5. The "I AM" Statements

In the book of John, Jesus uses the phrase "I AM" seven times to describe Himself. Look up these three and write what they mean to you.

- **John 8:12** ("I am the light of the world"):

- **John 10:11** ("I am the good shepherd"):

- **John 14:6** ("I am the way, the truth, and the life"):

  ----

6. Real-Life Application: Walking in His Steps

Pick one quality of Jesus that you saw in your reading this week (Example: He was kind to outcasts, He prayed often, He spoke the truth).

- **The Quality:**

- **The Plan:** How can you act like Jesus in this specific way at home or school tomorrow?

  ----

7. Guided Reflection Questions

Answer these briefly and directly.

- If Jesus were only a man and not God, why would His death not be enough to save everyone?

- If Jesus were only God and not a man, why would He not be able to understand your physical pain?

- Why is the resurrection (rising from the dead) the most important event in history?

  ----

8. The Exchange Check

Draw a line to match what Jesus took from us and what He gave back to us.

He Took: Our Sin	**He Gave:** His Peace
He Took: Our Shame	**He Gave:** His Righteousness (Perfection)
He Took: Our Death	**He Gave:** His Joy
He Took: Our Turmoil	**Gave:** His Eternal Life

9. Identifying Jesus in Your Day

Jesus said, "I am with you always."

* When did you feel like Jesus was "with you" today? (Example: During a hard test, while talking to a friend, while looking at nature).

----

10. Memory Verse Challenge

Memorize **John 1:14**: *"And the Word became flesh and dwelt among us, and we have seen his glory, glory as of the only Son from the Father, full of grace and truth."* Write it out here from memory:

----

11. A Letter to the Savior

Write a two-sentence "thank you" note to Jesus for what He did for you on the cross. Be specific about one thing He has changed in your life.

----

12. Final Action Step

Find one person this week who seems lonely or left out. Act as Jesus would by saying hello or including them.

Who will you look for?

----

13. Summary Question

Jesus asked His disciples, "Who do you say that I am?" If He asked you that question right now, what would your answer be?

CHAPTER 7

TRUST THE HELPER (PNEUMATOLOGY)

Read and Learn: How the Holy Spirit Gives You Strength and Peace

Imagine you are trying to build a massive skyscraper, but you only have a plastic hammer and a pair of scissors. No matter how hard you work, you simply do not have the power to finish the job. Many teens feel this way about their faith. They know what the Bible says, and they want to follow Jesus, but they feel like they lack the strength to actually do it. They try to be kind, but they get angry. They try to be pure, but their thoughts wander. They feel like they are running a race with no fuel in the tank.

The good news is that God did not leave you to live the Christian life on your own. When Jesus went back to heaven, He promised to send a "Helper." This Helper is the Holy Spirit. The study of the Holy Spirit is

165

called "Pneumatology." This comes from the Greek word *pneuma*, which means "wind," "breath," or "spirit." Just as you cannot see the wind but you can see what it moves, you cannot see the Holy Spirit, but you can see the powerful ways He moves in a person's life.

The first thing to understand is that the Holy Spirit is a Person. He is not a "force" like gravity or electricity. He is not an "it." He is the third Person of the Trinity. He has a mind, He has feelings, and He has a will. The Bible says we can grieve Him when we sin and we can talk to Him in prayer. Most importantly, if you have put your trust in Jesus, the Holy Spirit lives inside you right now. You are His home.

What does the Holy Spirit actually do? First, He is the one who "convicts" us. This means He is the one who taps you on the shoulder when you are about to do something wrong. He gives you that "gut feeling" that a certain movie is bad for you or that a joke you made was mean. He doesn't do this to make you feel guilty and miserable; He does it to lead you back to the truth. He is like a coach who points out a mistake so you can play better next time.

Second, the Holy Spirit "illuminates" the Word of God. Have you ever read a Bible verse that made no sense, but then suddenly, it clicked? That was the Holy Spirit. He is the author of the Bible, so He is the best one to explain it. He helps you see how an ancient story about a shepherd boy actually applies to your stress at school today.

Third, the Holy Spirit produces "fruit." In Galatians 5, the Bible says that as we walk with the Spirit, our lives start to grow things like love, joy, peace, patience, kindness, and self-control. You cannot "manufacture" these things by trying harder. You cannot force yourself to be truly joyful when everything is going wrong. But the Spirit can grow those traits in you from the inside out. He changes what you want, not just what you do.

Finally, the Spirit gives "gifts." These are special abilities given to every believer to help the church. Some people are given the gift of teaching, others the gift of encouragement, and others the gift of serving or leadership. You have a spiritual gift that your church needs. The Spirit empowers you to do things for God that you could never do by yourself.

Living with the Holy Spirit means you never have to walk alone. You have a constant Friend, a powerful Counselor, and a steady Guide. When you feel weak, He is your strength. When you feel confused, He is your peace. To trust the Helper, you simply have to stop trying to do everything in your own power and start asking Him for His.

This section is designed to help you recognize the work of the Spirit in your daily life and learn how to listen to His lead.

1. The "Fruit" Inspection

Read **Galatians 5:22-23**. Look at the nine fruits listed there.

- Which of these fruits is currently the most visible in your life?

  ____

  ____

- Which of these fruits do you feel is "missing" or struggling to grow?

  ____

  ____

- Why do you think that specific fruit is hard for you right now?

  ____

  ____

2. Identifying Conviction

Think about a time in the last week when you felt a "tug" in your heart telling you that you were doing something wrong.

- **The Situation:**

  ____

- **The Feeling:**

  ____

- **The Result:** Did you listen to that tug or ignore it? What happened next?

  ____

  ____

  ____

3. Word Study: The Paraclete

Jesus called the Holy Spirit the *Paraclete*. This is a Greek word that means "one who walks alongside."

- Imagine you are walking through a dark, dangerous forest. How would having a "Paraclete" (a guide walking right next to you) change your level of fear?

- How can you remind yourself that the Spirit is "walking alongside" you at school tomorrow?

  ----

4. Gifts vs. Talents

A "talent" is something you are born with (like being good at piano). A "spiritual gift" is something the Spirit gives you to help others know God.

- What is one natural talent you have?

- How could the Holy Spirit use that talent as a "gift" to serve your church?

  ----

5. The "Illumination" Test

Pick a verse from the Bible that you find confusing. Write it here:

Now, pray a short prayer asking the Holy Spirit to help you understand it. Read it again. What is one new thought or "lightbulb moment" you had about that verse?

----

6. Real-Life Application: Walking by the Spirit

Walking by the Spirit means checking in with God before you react.

- **The Challenge:** Tomorrow, before you post anything on social media or send a text, pause for five seconds. Ask, "Holy Spirit, does this reflect Your fruit?"
- **The Goal:** To let the Spirit filter your words before they leave your fingers.

7. Case Study: The Exhausted Volunteer

Sarah is helping with the kids' ministry at her church. She is tired, she has a lot of homework, and she feels like quitting. She is trying to be "kind" to the kids, but she is losing her temper.

- Is Sarah relying on her own power or the Spirit's power?

- What is one specific prayer Sarah could pray to the Holy Spirit in that moment?

  ----

8. Guided Reflection Questions

Answer these briefly and directly.

- Why is it important to remember that the Holy Spirit is a Person and not just a "vibe" or a "feeling"?

- How does the Holy Spirit help you when you don't know what to pray for? (See **Romans 8:26**).

- What does it mean to "grieve" the Holy Spirit? (See **Ephesians 4:30**).

----

9. True or False?
- The Holy Spirit only comes to "super-Christians" or pastors.   (_______)
- You can have the Holy Spirit and still struggle with sin.   (_______)
- The Spirit's job is to make us look more like Jesus.   (_______)
- The Holy Spirit is less important than God the Father.   (_______)

10. Memory Verse Challenge

Memorize **Acts 1:8**: *"But you will receive power when the Holy Spirit has come upon you, and you will be my witnesses..."* Write the verse below and circle the word "power."

----

11. Identifying the Spirit's Voice

The Spirit usually speaks through the Bible or a quiet peace in our hearts. He never contradicts the Bible.

- If you have an idea to do something that the Bible says is wrong, is that the Holy Spirit speaking?

----

12. A Prayer for the Helper

"Holy Spirit, thank You for living in me. I admit that I have been trying to live in my own strength. Please grow Your fruit in my heart today. Help me to hear Your voice and give me the power to obey. Amen."

13. Final Thought

If the same Spirit who raised Jesus from the dead lives in you, is there any temptation in your life that is too strong for Him to beat?

CHAPTER 8

WALK IN SALVATION (SOTERIOLOGY)

Read and Learn: How Grace Changes Your Past, Present, and Future

In the world of sports, you have to earn your spot on the team. You have to practice hard, show up on time, and perform better than the next person. In school, you have to study to earn a good grade. Most of our lives are built on "if-then" systems: **if** you do the work, **then** you get the reward. Because of this, many people think God works the same way. They think they have to be "good enough" for God to like them. They hope that at the end of their lives, their good deeds will outweigh their bad ones.

But Christian theology teaches something completely different. This is the study of "Soteriology," which comes from the Greek word *soter*, meaning "savior" or "deliverer." It is the study of how God rescues us.

The most important thing to know about salvation is that it is a gift, not a paycheck. You do not earn it; you accept it.

Salvation happens in three "stages." Think of it as your past, your present, and your future.

First, there is **Justification**. This happens the very moment you put your faith in Jesus. In a courtroom, a judge might declare someone "not guilty." But God goes even further. He declares you "righteous." He takes your sin and gives you the perfection of Jesus. It is as if you have never sinned and have always obeyed. This solves your "past" problem. Your debt is paid, and you are officially a child of God. You are saved from the **penalty** of sin.

Second, there is **Sanctification**. This is what is happening right now. Once you are saved, God doesn't just leave you where you are. He begins a process of changing you from the inside out. He helps you hate the things He hates and love the things He loves. This is a slow process. You will still mess up, and you will still struggle. But over time, you should look more like Jesus than you did a year ago. You are being saved from the **power** of sin.

Third, there is **Glorification**. This is your future. When Jesus returns or when you go to be with Him after death, your struggle with sin will be over. You will receive a new body that never gets sick, and a heart that never wants to sin. You will be saved from the **presence** of sin.

How do you receive this gift? The Bible is very clear: it is by grace through faith. Grace means getting something good that you do not deserve. Faith is not just "believing that God exists." Even the demons believe that. Faith is **trust**. It is like sitting in a chair. You don't just believe the chair exists; you put your full weight on it. To have faith in Jesus means you stop trusting in your own "goodness" and put your full weight on what He did on the cross.

Many teens worry they can "lose" their salvation if they have a bad week. But if you didn't earn your salvation by being good, you can't lose it by being bad. Salvation is held together by God's power, not your effort. Because He started the work in you, He is the one who will finish it. This gives you the freedom to serve God out of love, not out of fear. You don't obey to **get** saved; you obey because you **are** saved.

This section is about moving salvation from a "head idea" to a "heart reality."

1. The Three Tenses of Salvation

Based on what you read, fill in the blanks below to see how God is working in your life.

- **Past:** I have been saved from the ________ of sin. (Justification)
- **Present:** I am being saved from the ________ of sin. (Sanctification)
- **Future:** I will be saved from the ________ of sin. (Glorification)

2. Grace vs. Merit

- **Merit:** Working a job for 10 hours and receiving $150.
- **Grace:** Having a debt of $1,000,000 and someone else paying it for you while giving you a gift on top of it.
- Which one describes your relationship with God?

  ____

  ____

- How does this make you feel about your "mistakes" from last week?

  ____

  ____

3. The "Chair" Test of Faith

Read **Ephesians 2:8-9**.

- According to these verses, can you brag about being a Christian? Why or why not?

  ____

  ____

- If salvation is a gift, what is the only thing you have to do to receive it?

  ____

  ____

4. Your Faith Story (Testimony)

A "testimony" is just a story of how you met Jesus. Even if it isn't "dramatic," it is powerful. Write one sentence for each part:

- **Before:** What was your life or attitude like before you trusted Jesus (or when you were younger)?

- **How:** How did you realize you needed a Savior?

- **After:** What is one way your life is different now that you know Him?

    ----

5. Practice the "Bridge" Illustration

Draw a simple picture here. On one side is a cliff labeled "People/Sin." On the other side is a cliff labeled "God/Holy." In the middle is a deep gap.

- How does Jesus act as the bridge between the two?

- Why can't we "jump" across the gap on our own?

    ----

6. Real-Life Application: The Assurance Check

Read **1 John 5:11-13**.

- Does God want you to "guess" if you are saved or "know" that you are saved?

- What is the "evidence" mentioned in verse 12?

    ----

7. Case Study: The "Good Guy" Friend

Your friend Alex is a great person. He is kind, gets straight A's, and volunteers. He says, "I don't need Jesus. I'm a good person, and God will see that."

- Based on **Romans 3:23** and what you learned about Justification, what is Alex missing?

- How could you kindly explain that even "good" people need a Savior?

  ----

8. Guided Reflection Questions

- If you knew for 100% certain that God would never leave you, how would that change the way you pray when you mess up?

- What is the difference between "feeling" saved and "being" saved?

  ----

9. True or False?

- Faith means I never have doubts.   (_______)
- Justification is a one-time event.   (_______)
- Sanctification is a process that takes a lifetime.   (_______)
- I have to do more good things than bad things to
  go to heaven.   (_______)

10. Memory Verse Challenge

Memorize **Romans 10:9**: *"Because, if you confess with your mouth that Jesus is Lord and believe in your heart that God raised him from the dead, you will be saved."* Write it out below:

----

11. A Prayer of Thanks

"Lord, thank You that my salvation does not depend on my performance. Thank You for the gift of Jesus. I trust Him as my Savior and my King. Help me to live this week out of gratitude for what You have already done. Amen."

12. Final Action Step

This week, tell one person (a parent, a friend, or a mentor) one thing you learned about God's grace.

- **Who will you tell?**

CHAPTER 9

SERVE THE CHURCH (ECCLESIOLOGY)

Read and Learn: Why the Church is a Team That Needs Your Help

When you hear the word "church," what is the first thing you picture? For some, it is a building with a tall steeple and stained-glass windows. For others, it is a boring hour on a Sunday morning where you have to wear uncomfortable clothes and sit still. Many people today think the church is an optional social club, something you attend if you have extra time or if your parents make you go. They see it as a place to "get" something: a good message, some music, or a chance to see friends.

But in the Bible, the church is never described as a building or a weekly event. The study of the church is called "Ecclesiology," from the Greek word *ekklesia*, which means "a called-out assembly." The church is a group of people who have been called out of the world to belong to

Jesus. It is not a place you go; it is a family you belong to. It is not a performance you watch; it is a team you play on.

The Bible uses several powerful pictures to describe what the church is. One of the most famous is the **Body of Christ**. In 1 Corinthians 12, the apostle Paul explains that just as a human body has many parts, eyes, ears, hands, and feet, the church has many members. Each part has a different job, but every part is necessary. If the whole body were an eye, how would it hear? If the whole body were an ear, how would it smell? This means that you are a vital "organ" in the body of Jesus. If you are not there, or if you are not "functioning," the whole body suffers. You aren't just a spectator; you are a limb.

Another picture is the **Family of God**. When you trust in Jesus, God becomes your Father, which makes every other believer your brother or sister. This is why we often call people in church "Brother" or "Sister." This family is bigger than your DNA. It includes people of every age, every race, and every background. In a world where people are increasingly lonely, the church is meant to be a place where you are known, loved, and protected. You have "spiritual parents" to give you wisdom and "spiritual siblings" to walk through life with you.

The church is also called the **Temple of the Holy Spirit**. In the Old Testament, God's presence lived in a physical building made of stone and gold. Today, God lives in His people. When we gather together, God is present in a special way. We are like "living stones" being built into a house where God dwells. This makes the church holy and important. It is the place where heaven meets earth.

So, why does the church exist? It has a few main "assignments."

1. **Worship:** We gather to tell God how great He is.
2. **Discipleship:** We help each other grow in the Word and become more like Jesus.
3. **Fellowship:** We care for each other's needs, pray for each other, and eat together.
4. **Mission:** We work together to tell the world the Good News about salvation.

You might wonder, "Do I really need the local church? Can't I just follow Jesus on my own?" The answer from the Bible is a clear "no." You cannot be a "lone wolf" Christian. A coal that is pulled out of the fire quickly goes cold. To stay on fire for God, you need the heat of other believers around you. You need people to encourage you when you are down and people to correct you when you start to wander away from the truth.

The local church also has a specific structure. God provides **pastors** and **elders** to lead and protect the "flock." He provides **deacons** to serve and meet practical needs. These leaders are there to "equip" you. Their job isn't to do all the work of the ministry; their job is to train *you* to do the work. Whether you are 13 or 30, you have a role to play.

Serving the church is one of the best ways to grow your faith. When you stop focusing on yourself and start focusing on helping others, you start to see God work in amazing ways. You might help in the nursery, run the soundboard, help set up chairs, or welcome visitors at the door. No job is too small for a servant of the King. When you serve, you aren't just helping the church; you are serving Jesus Himself.

The church is not perfect because it is filled with people like you and me—people who still struggle with sin. You will likely be let down by someone in a church at some point. You might find a service boring or a leader frustrating. But we don't give up on the church because it's imperfect. We stay committed because Jesus is committed to it. He calls the church His "Bride." He loves her, He died for her, and He is coming back for her. If the church is that important to Jesus, it should be that important to us.

Apply and Act: Pick a Way to Help Your Church Family This Week

This section will help you move from being a "customer" at church to being a "contributor."

1. The Body Part Inventory

In 1 Corinthians 12, Paul says every part of the body is important.

- If you had to describe yourself as a part of the body right now, which would you be? (Example: The "feet" because I like to go and do things; the "ears" because I am a good listener).

- Why did you pick that part?

----

2. Identifying Your Local Family

- Write down the name of your local church:

- Who are two adults in your church (besides your parents) that you look up to?

- Have you ever told them you appreciate them? If not, plan to do so this Sunday.

----

3. Word Study: Koinonia

The Bible uses the Greek word *koinonia* to describe the "fellowship" of the church. It means "sharing things in common."

- List three things you share in common with other people in your youth group or church.

----

4. The "One Another" Challenge

The New Testament has over 50 "one another" commands (e.g., "Love one another," "Encourage one another," "Pray for one another").

- Read **Hebrews 10:24-25.**
- According to these verses, what is the main reason we should not stop meeting together?

- How can you "stir up" a friend to do good works this week?

----

5. Service Scavenger Hunt

Look at the different ministries in your church. Put a checkmark next to any area where a teen could potentially help.

- [   ] Greeting/Welcoming people
- [   ] Helping with younger children
- [   ] Setting up or cleaning up events
- [   ] Music or Tech/Audio-Visual
- [   ] Cleaning the building or yard
- [   ] Visiting older members or sending cards

6. Real-Life Application: The First-Time Visitor Perspective

Imagine you are walking into your church for the very first time. You don't know anyone and you don't know where to go.

- What is one thing a teen in the church could do to make you feel welcome?

- Will you commit to doing that the next time you see someone new?

  ----

7. Case Study: The "I'm Bored" Dilemma

Your friend Tyler says, "I hate going to church. The music is old, the sermon is too long, and I don't get anything out of it. I'd rather just watch a YouTube preacher at home."

- Based on the "Body of Christ" idea, what is Tyler missing by staying home?

- How would you explain to Tyler that church isn't about "getting" something, but about "giving" something?

  ----

8. Guided Reflection Questions

- Why is it dangerous to think you can be a Christian without being part of a local church?

- How does the church act as a "hospital" for people who are hurting?

- What is one way your church could reach out to your school or neighborhood?

----

9. True or False?

- The church is a building where God lives. (_______)
- You are an important part of the body of Christ right now. (_______)
- Only pastors and elders are responsible for doing ministry. (_______)
- The church is a global family of all believers throughout history. (_______)

10. Memory Verse Challenge

- Memorize **1 Corinthians 12:27**: *"Now you are the body of Christ and individually members of it."* Write it out three times below:

----

11. The "Ask Your Pastor" Task

This week, find a leader at your church and ask them this question: "Is there a small way I can help out or serve this month?"

- **Who will you ask?**

- **What was their answer?**

  ----

12. A Prayer for Your Church

"Father, thank You for my church family. Thank You that I don't have to follow Jesus alone. Please protect our leaders and help us to love one another well. Show me where I can help and how I can use my gifts to serve You. Amen."

13. Final Thought

If the church is the "Bride of Christ," how should that change the way you talk about the church to your friends?

CHAPTER 10

CHANGE YOUR LIFE (SANCTIFICATION)

Read and Learn: How to Grow in Holiness by Following God's Rules

If you have ever started a workout routine or tried to learn a new language, you know that the first day is very different from the hundredth day. On day one, you make a decision. You sign the contract, you buy the shoes, or you download the app. But on day one hundred, you are a different person. Your muscles are stronger, or your vocabulary is larger. The initial decision was a one-time event, but the growth is a long-term process.

In your walk with God, something similar happens. In Chapter 8, we talked about *Justification*, that one-time event where God declares you "not guilty" because of Jesus. But once you are on the team, God begins the work of training you. This process is called **Sanctification**. It comes from the word "sanctify," which means to set something apart or to make it holy. Sanctification is the lifelong journey of becoming in your daily life what God has already declared you to be in His courtroom.

Sanctification is unique because it is a "cooperative" work. When it came to your salvation, Jesus did 100% of the work. You didn't help Him die on the cross, and you didn't help yourself be born again. However, in sanctification, God works and *you* work. The apostle Paul describes it this way: "Work out your own salvation with fear and trembling, for it is God who works in you" (Philippians 2:12-13). God provides the "want-to" and the power, but you have to provide the "do." You have to make the choices. You have to say "no" to the old habits and "yes" to the new ones.

So, how does this change actually happen? It isn't magic, and it usually doesn't happen overnight. God uses "means of grace", tools He has given us to help us grow.

1. The Word of God You cannot grow in holiness if you don't know what holiness looks like. The Bible acts as a light that shows you where the obstacles are. Jesus prayed, "Sanctify them in the truth; your word is truth" (John 17:17). As you read the Bible, it starts to scrub your mind. You stop seeing things through the world's eyes and start seeing them through God's eyes.

2. The Holy Spirit As we learned in Chapter 7, the Spirit is the "Helper." He is the engine of sanctification. He gives you a "holy nudge" when you are about to lose your temper. He gives you a sense of peace when you choose to tell the truth even when it's hard. Without the Spirit, sanctification is just "moralism", trying to be a good person to impress people. With the Spirit, it is a transformation of the heart.

3. Discipline and Habits Sanctification requires effort. This is where "God's rules" come in. We don't follow God's rules to *become* His children; we follow them because we *are* His children. Think of God's commands like the guardrails on a mountain road. They aren't there to stop you from having fun; they are there to keep you from driving off a cliff. When you practice disciplines like prayer, fasting, and church attendance, you are creating a space where God can change you.

4. Trials and Hard Times This is the part we usually don't like. Sometimes God uses difficult situations to "burn away" the things in us that shouldn't be there. Just as gold is heated in a fire to remove the dirt (impurities), our faith is often tested to make us stronger and more patient. When you face a hard time at school or a disappointment at home, God can use that to help you trust Him more than you trust yourself.

It is important to remember that sanctification is not about being "perfect." You will still have bad days. You will still struggle with the same sins you thought you defeated months ago. The goal of sanctification is not "perfection" in this life, but "direction." Is the general direction of your life moving toward Jesus? Are you more bothered by your sin today than you were last year? Do you love God more now than you used to?

A key part of this change is the "Put Off / Put On" principle found in Ephesians 4. Paul tells us to "put off" our old self, the lying, the anger, the selfishness, and to "put on" the new self, the truth-telling, the kindness, the hard work. You can't just stop a bad habit; you have to replace it with a good one. If you stop gossiping but don't start using your words to encourage people, there will be a hole in your heart that the gossip will eventually fill back up.

Change is hard, but you aren't doing it alone. The God who started the work in you is committed to finishing it. Every time you choose to be kind when you want to be mean, or honest when you want to lie, you are winning a small battle in the long war of sanctification. Keep going. The change is worth it.

Apply and Act: Set New Daily Habits That Honor God

Sanctification is about what you do when no one is looking. Use these exercises to build a plan for growth.

1. The "Direction" Check

Think about your life one year ago compared to today.

- What is one way you have grown in your faith?

  ____

  ____

- What is one sin or habit that you struggle with *less* now than you did then?

- What is one area where you feel "stuck"?

  ----

2. Put Off and Put On

Identify a "weed" in your heart (a bad habit) and a "seed" you want to plant (a good habit).

Put Off (The Weed)	Put On (The Seed)
Example: Complaining about school	*Example: Thanking God for the chance to learn*

3. Designing a "Rule of Life"

A "Rule of Life" is just a schedule of habits that keep you close to God. Fill in a simple plan for your week:

- **Daily:** When will I read the Bible and pray?

- **Weekly:** How will I serve or worship with others?

- **Monthly:** Is there something I can give up (like a fast from social media) to focus on God?

----

4. Word Study: Holiness

The word "Holy" (*hagios* in Greek) means "different" or "set apart."

- What is one thing you do during your week that makes you look "different" from your friends who don't follow Jesus?

- Is being "different" in that way a good thing or a bad thing? Why?

----

5. The "Means of Grace" Inventory

Which of these tools are you using the most right now? Which one do you need to pick up?

- [   ] **The Word:** I read it consistently.
- [   ] **Prayer:** I talk to God throughout the day.
- [   ] **Fellowship:** I have friends who push me toward Jesus.
- [   ] **The Sacraments:** I participate in Baptism and the Lord's Supper.

6. Real-Life Application: The Five-Minute Morning

For the next seven days, commit to spending the first five minutes of your day without your phone.

- **Minute 1-2:** Thank God for three specific things.

- **Minute 3-4:** Read a short Psalm.

- **Minute 5:** Ask the Holy Spirit to lead your choices today.

- **Check back:** How did this change your mood by lunchtime?

  ----

7. Case Study: The "Frustrated Christian"

Mark has been a Christian for two years. He is frustrated because he still gets angry very easily. He feels like he isn't "changing" enough, so he feels like giving up on church.

- Based on the "Direction vs. Perfection" idea, what would you say to Mark?

- How does knowing that sanctification is a "lifelong journey" help Mark?

  ----

8. Guided Reflection Questions

- Why does God give us "rules" or commands if we are already saved by grace?

- What is the difference between "trying" to be holy and "training" to be holy?

- How do your friends influence your sanctification (your growth in holiness)?

  ----

9. Identifying the Resistance

What is the biggest "distraction" that keeps you from growing spiritually? (Example: Gaming, social media, sports, sleep).

How can you put a "guardrail" around that distraction this week?

----

10. Memory Verse Challenge

Memorize **1 Thessalonians 4:3**: *"For this is the will of God, your sanctification..."* Write it out three times and keep it in your pocket today.

----

11. The "Holy" Habit Tracker

Pick one small habit (like praying before you eat or reading one verse before bed). Mark a checkbox for every day you do it this week.

- M   [ ]
- T   [ ]
- W   [ ]
- T   [ ]
- F   [ ]
- S   [ ]
- S   [ ]

12. A Prayer for Growth

"Lord, I want to change. I don't want to stay the same person I am today. Thank You for loving me as I am, but thank You for not leaving me as I am. Please give me the strength to put off my old selfish ways and put on Your love and truth. Make me holy, as You are holy. Amen."

13. Final Thought

If sanctification is a team effort between you and God, who is responsible if you aren't growing? Who is responsible for the power to grow?

CHAPTER 11

FACE THE ENEMY (ANGELOLOGY/SPIRITUAL WARFARE)

Read and Learn: Understanding the Unseen World and Finding Victory

Most of the time, we focus only on what we can see: our friends, our homework, our phones, and our families. But the Bible tells us that there is an entire world existing right alongside ours that is completely invisible to the human eye. This is the spiritual realm. Just because you can't see it doesn't mean it isn't real. In fact, the things happening in the unseen world often drive the things happening in the visible world.

The study of this realm is called **Angelology** (the study of angels) and **Demonology** (the study of fallen angels). Understanding this isn't about being scared or becoming obsessed with ghost stories. It's about being prepared. If you were walking into a literal battlefield but didn't believe there was an enemy, you would be in serious trouble.

The Good Guys: Angels

Angels are created spiritual beings. They are not "humans who died and got wings." They were created before the world began to serve God and care for His people. They are incredibly powerful, intelligent, and fast. The Bible shows them doing several things:

- **Worshiping God:** They constantly surround God's throne, singing of His holiness.

- **Delivering Messages:** The word "angel" literally means "messenger." They brought the news of Jesus' birth and told the disciples He had risen.

- **Protecting Believers:** Psalm 91 says God commands His angels to guard you. They often step in to help us in ways we don't even realize until later.

The Bad Guys: Demons and Satan

Not all spiritual beings stayed on God's side. Long ago, a high-ranking angel named Lucifer (Satan) became proud. He wanted to be God rather than serve God. He led a rebellion, and a third of the angels fell with him. These are now known as demons.

Satan is not God's equal. He is a created being, which means he is on a leash. He is not all-knowing or all-powerful. However, he is a master of deception. The Bible calls him the "Father of Lies" and the "Accuser." His goal is simple: to steal, kill, and destroy. He wants to destroy your relationship with God, your reputation, and your joy.

The Battle: Spiritual Warfare

Because you belong to Jesus, you are a target. This isn't meant to frighten you, but to wake you up. You are in a spiritual war. However, this war isn't fought with tanks and guns. It is fought in your mind and your heart.

The "front lines" of spiritual warfare usually look like:

- **Lies:** The enemy whispers that you aren't good enough, that God is holding out on you, or that "just once" won't hurt.

- **Discouragement:** Making you feel like giving up on your faith or your church.

- **Division:** Stirring up drama between you and your parents or friends.

The Victory: The Armor of God

In Ephesians 6, the Bible tells us exactly how to fight back. We are told to "put on the full armor of God."

1. **The Belt of Truth:** Knowing what God says is true so you can spot the enemy's lies.

2. **The Breastplate of Righteousness:** Protecting your heart by living a life that honors God.

3. **The Shoes of Peace:** Being ready to share the Gospel and staying calm in the chaos.

4. **The Shield of Faith:** Trusting God's promises to "extinguish" the flaming arrows of doubt.

5. **The Helmet of Salvation:** Protecting your mind by remembering you belong to Jesus.

6. **The Sword of the Spirit:** The Word of God. This is your only offensive weapon. When Jesus was tempted by Satan, He didn't argue; He quoted Scripture.

The most important thing to remember is that the war is already won. Jesus defeated Satan at the cross. The enemy is like a defeated army that is still causing trouble as it retreats. You don't fight *for* victory; you fight *from* victory. Because the Holy Spirit is in you, you have more power than any demon in existence. "He who is in you is greater than he who is in the world" (1 John 4:4).

Apply and Act: Recognize the Lies and Put on Your Armor

This section helps you move from being a victim of the enemy's schemes to being a soldier in God's kingdom.

1. Identifying the "Arrows"

Satan often uses "flaming arrows" of thoughts to get us off track. Which of these "arrows" have you felt this week? (Check all that apply).

- [ ] "God is disappointed in you because of what you did."
- [ ] "You're the only one who actually cares about this stuff."
- [ ] "One little lie won't matter; everyone does it."
- [ ] "You'll never be as good a Christian as [Name]."
- [ ] "Is the Bible even really true?"

2. Using the Sword

Pick one of the arrows you checked above. Find a "Sword" (a Bible verse) that cuts through that lie.

- **The Lie:**

- **The Truth (Bible Verse):**

  ----

3. The Reality Check

Read **2 Kings 6:15-17**.

- What did Elisha's servant see at first?

- What did he see after Elisha prayed for his eyes to be opened?

- How does this story change how you feel when you feel "outnumbered" at school?

  ----

4. Word Study: The Accuser

The name "Satan" actually means "Accuser." He likes to remind you of your sins to make you feel too dirty to pray.

- Read **Romans 8:1**. If you are in Christ, is there any condemnation left for you?

- Next time you feel "accused" of a past sin, what will you tell the enemy?

  ----

5. Daily Armor Drill

Before you leave the house tomorrow, literally go through the motions of putting on the armor.

- **The Belt:** "God, help me speak and believe the truth today."
- **The Breastplate:** "Protect my heart from doing things I know are wrong."
- **The Shoes:** "Make me a peacemaker at school today."
- **The Shield:** "I trust You even if things get hard today."
- **The Helmet:** "Thank You that I am saved and I am Yours."
- **The Sword:** "Remind me of Your Word when I am tempted."

6. Case Study: The "Just a Little" Temptation

Your friends are planning to sneak out or do something you know your parents wouldn't allow. You feel a massive amount of pressure to go. You start thinking, "God will forgive me anyway, and I want to have fun."

- Is this just your thought, or could it be a spiritual attack?

  ____

  ____

- Which piece of armor do you need most in this moment?

  ____

  ____

- What is the "Sword of the Spirit" (verse) you can use to stay strong?

  ____

  ____

7. Guided Reflection Questions

- Why is it dangerous to be *too* afraid of the devil?

  ____

  ____

- Why is it dangerous to *ignore* the reality of the devil?

  ____

  ____

- What is the difference between an angel and a human?

----

8. True or False?

- Angels are the spirits of people who have died.   (________)
- Satan can read your mind.   (________)
- We have the power to defeat the enemy because of Jesus.   (________)
- Spiritual warfare is mostly about scary movies and exorcisms.   (________)

9. Identifying the "Strongholds"

A "stronghold" is a pattern of thinking that is hard to break. (Example: "I have to be perfect for people to like me.")

- Is there a "stronghold" in your mind that the enemy uses to keep you unhappy?

- How can the "Truth" (the Belt) set you free from that?

----

10. Memory Verse Challenge

Memorize **James 4:7**: *"Submit yourselves therefore to God. Resist the devil, and he will flee from you."* Note the order: you must submit to God *before* you can successfully resist the devil. Write it here:

----

11. A Prayer for Protection

"Lord, thank You that the victory is already Yours. I put on Your armor today. Protect my mind from lies and my heart from evil. Send Your angels to guard me and my family. Help me to stand firm in my faith and to use Your Word to fight back against temptation. Amen."

12. Final Thought

If you are on the winning team, why do we sometimes act like we are losing? How can you live like a "victor" this week?

CHAPTER 12

WAIT FOR THE KING (ESCHATOLOGY)

Read and Learn: Why the End of the Story is the Best Part

If you have ever read a long book or watched a movie series, you know that the ending is what gives the whole story meaning. If a hero dies for no reason, or if the villain wins and everyone stays sad, the story feels broken. But if the hero returns, the broken things are fixed, and the characters find a home, the ending makes the earlier struggles worth it.

The study of the "end times" or the "last things" is called **Eschatology**. It comes from the Greek word *eschatos*, which means "last." For many people, this topic feels scary. They think about world-ending disasters, mysterious beasts, and a "Great Tribulation." But for a follower of Jesus, eschatology isn't a horror movie. It is a love story. It is the promise that the King who left is coming back to claim His people and set the world right.

The Return of the King

The most important event in the future is the **Second Coming of Christ**. When Jesus left the earth after His resurrection, the angels told the disciples, "This Jesus, who was taken up from you into heaven, will come in the same way as you saw him go into heaven" (Acts 1:11).

Unlike His first coming, where He arrived as a quiet baby in a humble manger, His second coming will be loud, visible, and unmistakable. Every eye will see Him. He is not coming back to be judged; He is coming back to judge. He is not coming back to die; He is coming back to rule. For those who love Him, this is the most exciting day in history. It means that the war with sin and the devil is finally over.

The Resurrection of the Body

One of the most amazing parts of eschatology is what happens to *us*. The Bible teaches that when Jesus returns, there will be a "resurrection of the dead." This doesn't mean we will be floating clouds or ghosts in white robes. It means our physical bodies will be brought back to life, but they will be better.

In 1 Corinthians 15, Paul calls our current bodies "seeds." A seed is small and brown, but when it grows, it becomes a beautiful flower or a strong tree. Our "resurrection bodies" will be like Jesus' body after He rose. We will be able to eat, walk, and talk, but we will never get sick, we will never grow old, and we will never die again. The "brokenness" you feel in your body or your mind today is temporary.

The Final Judgment

The Bible is also honest about the fact that there is a day of accounting. God is a perfectly just Judge. He cannot let evil go unpunished forever. There will be a Final Judgment where every secret is brought into the light.

- **For those who rejected Jesus:** This is a day of great sadness. Without the "bridge" of Jesus (which we talked about in Chapter 8), they must pay the penalty for their own sins, which is eternal separation from God in a place the Bible calls Hell.

- **For those who trust Jesus:** This is not a day of fear. Because Jesus already took their punishment on the cross, they are welcomed into the Kingdom. Their "works" will be tested, not to see if they get into heaven, but to receive rewards for how they served God.

A New Heaven and a New Earth

Many people think that "Heaven" is just a place in the clouds where we sit on harps. But the Bible's ending is much better than that. In Revelation 21, John sees a "New Heaven and a New Earth." God is going to "make all things new."

Imagine the most beautiful place you have ever been—a mountain lake, a lush forest, or a perfect sunset. Now, imagine that place without any trash, any pollution, any sadness, or any mosquitoes! The New Earth will be a physical world where we live with God. There will be no more cancer, no more school shootings, no more depression, and no more funerals. "He will wipe away every tear from their eyes, and death shall be no more" (Revelation 21:4).

How Do We Wait?

Since we know the ending, how should we live today? We shouldn't be obsessed with trying to guess the exact date Jesus will return (Jesus said even He didn't know the day or hour!). Instead, we should live with **Urgency** and **Hope**.

- **Urgency:** We want to tell our friends about Jesus now, because we know the story has an end.

- **Hope:** When we go through hard times, bullying, family problems, or health issues, we remember that the "best part" hasn't started yet. We are like people standing in the rain who know that a warm house and a feast are waiting for them just around the corner.

The very last prayer in the Bible is simple: *"Amen. Come, Lord Jesus!"* (Revelation 22:20). That should be our prayer too.

Eschatology is meant to change your "now," not just your "later." Use these activities to focus your heart on the coming King.

1. The "Wipe Away" List

Read **Revelation 21:1-5**.

- List three things that exist in our world today that will *not* exist in the New Earth.

  1. ____

  2. ____

  3. ____

- Which one are you most excited to see gone? Why?

  ____

  ____

2. Word Study: Maranatha

In the early church, Christians used the word "Maranatha" as a greeting. It is an Aramaic word that means "Our Lord, come!"

- Why do you think people today are sometimes *afraid* for Jesus to come back?

- How can you shift your mindset from "I'm scared of the end" to "Maranatha"?

3. The "Resurrection Body" Reflection

If you could ask God for one thing to be "healed" or "fixed" in your resurrection body (a disability, a scar, a mental struggle), what would it be?

____

____

Take a moment to thank God that a day is coming when that struggle will be gone forever.

4. Identifying the Signs

Jesus gave us some "birth pains" to look for that show the end is approaching (Matthew 24).

- [   ] Wars and rumors of wars
- [   ] Famines and earthquakes
- [   ] People's love growing cold
- [   ] The Gospel being preached to all nations
- Do you see any of these happening in the news today?

----

5. Real-Life Application: Living with Urgency

If you knew for a fact that Jesus was returning this Friday, what is one thing you would do differently this week?

- Why wait until the end? Can you do that one thing *this* week?

----

6. Case Study: The "Depressed" Christian

Your friend Chloe is going through a really hard time. Her parents are getting a divorce, and she says, "Everything is falling apart. There's no point in trying because the world is just going to get worse anyway."

- How does the "New Heaven and New Earth" promise give Chloe a reason to keep going?

- How would you explain that our suffering today is "light and momentary" compared to the glory that is coming? (See **2 Corinthians 4:17**).

----

7. The Reward System

Read **1 Corinthians 3:12-15**.

- The Bible says our work for God is like "gold, silver, and precious stones." What is one "work" you did this week that you think God would consider "precious"? (Example: Helping a sibling, praying for a teacher).

----

8. Guided Reflection Questions

- What is the difference between "Heaven" and the "New Earth"?

- Why is it important that Jesus comes back *physically* and not just "in our hearts"?

- How does knowing the end of the story help you when you see bad news on the internet?

----

9. True or False?

- We will become angels when we die.   (________)
- No one knows the exact date when Jesus will return.   (________)
- The New Earth will be a place where we can do physical activities like eating and working.   (________)
- Hell is a place of eternal separation from God.   (________)

10. Memory Verse Challenge

Memorize **Revelation 21:4**: *"He will wipe away every tear from their eyes, and death shall be no more, neither shall there be mourning, nor crying, nor pain anymore, for the former things have passed away."* Write it out here:

----

11. The "Kingdom" Habit

Jesus told us to pray, "Your Kingdom come, Your will be done, on earth as it is in heaven."

- What is one way you can bring a "little bit of heaven" to your school or home today? (Example: Being a peacemaker in an argument).

____

____

12. A Prayer for the Return

"Lord Jesus, thank You that the story doesn't end with sin and death. Thank You that You are coming back to fix every broken thing. Help me to live with hope today. Give me the courage to tell others about Your Kingdom. We join the voices of the saints and say: Maranatha! Come, Lord Jesus! Amen."

13. Final Thought

At the end of the Bible, God says, "Behold, I am making all things new." What is the one thing in your life you most want Him to make new?

____

____

____

____

____

____

CONCLUSION

KEEP GOING

Read and Learn: The End of the Book is the Beginning of the Journey

Congratulations. You have arrived at the final pages of this journey. If you have read through the previous twelve chapters, you have done something that many adults never do: you have built a systematic framework for your faith. You have traveled from the mountaintop of *Theology Proper* (who God is) to the valley of *Hamartiology* (the problem of sin), and you have looked forward to the glorious sunrise of *Eschatology* (the return of the King). You now possess a map of the Christian faith. You know where the roads lead, where the dangers lie, and where the treasure is buried.

However, there is a massive difference between owning a map and actually taking the trip. You can study a map of Paris for years—memorizing the street names, the location of the Eiffel Tower, and the best places to get a croissant—but until you actually step onto a plane and walk the streets, you haven't truly experienced Paris. In the same way, theology is the map, but the Christian life is the journey. You have spent this time studying the map so that you can walk the road with confidence. But the map is not the destination. God is the destination.

This conclusion is not really an ending; it is a commissioning. It is a "send-off." In graduation ceremonies, the final speech is often called the "Commencement Address." "Commencement" means "beginning." You are graduating from this basic study, but you are commencing a lifetime of walking with Jesus. As you close this book and step back into your normal life—with its homework, social drama, sports practices, and family dynamics—there are several critical truths you must carry with you to ensure that you don't just *start* well, but that you *keep going*.

The Danger of the "Big Head, Small Heart"

The first danger you face now that you know some theology is pride. The Bible warns us in 1 Corinthians 8:1 that "knowledge puffs up, but love builds up." There is a trap that many young theologians fall into. They learn big words like *Justification, Inerrancy,* and *Omniscience*. They learn the arguments against atheism and the errors of other religions. And suddenly, they feel superior. They start to use their theology like a club to beat people over the head rather than a light to guide them home.

You might find yourself sitting in a small group or a Sunday school class, listening to someone say something that isn't *quite* theologically correct. The temptation will be to jump in, correct them, and show off what you know. But remember this: The devil is a better theologian than you are. He knows the Bible better than you do. He knows exactly who Jesus is (James 2:19 says the demons believe and shudder). The difference is that the devil has a massive amount of knowledge and zero love. He has a big head and a shriveled heart.

True theology should always lead to *Doxology* (worship) and *Missiology* (mission). If your study of God makes you love people less, you have studied wrong. If learning about God's holiness makes you arrogant rather than humble, you have missed the point. As you move forward, check your heart. Is your knowledge fueling your love? Are you becoming kinder, more patient, and more gracious? The greatest theologians in history were not the ones who won the most debates; they were the ones who looked the most like Jesus.

The Spiral of Faith: Learning the Same Truths Deeper

One of the misconceptions about growing in faith is that you "master" a topic and move on. You might think, "I already did Chapter 2 on God's attributes. I know that God is love. What's next?" But the Christian life is not a straight line where you leave the basics behind. It is a spiral. You circle back to the same truths over and over again, but each time, you go deeper.

- **Level 1:** When you are 5 years old, you learn "Jesus loves me." It makes you feel safe in the dark.

- **Level 2:** When you are 15 (right now), you learn "Jesus loves me" means He died on the cross to pay for your sins (Atonement). It helps you deal with guilt and shame.

- **Level 3:** When you are 25 and perhaps face a career failure or a broken engagement, you will need to learn "Jesus loves me" in a new way—that His love is your identity, not your success.

- **Level 4:** When you are 50 and perhaps lose a parent or face a health crisis, "Jesus loves me" will become the rock that keeps you from despair.

- **Level 5:** When you are on your deathbed, "Jesus loves me" will be the only thing that matters as you prepare to meet Him.

It is the same truth, but the depth is infinite. Never feel like you are "too advanced" for the basics. The Gospel is not the ABCs of Christianity; it is the A to Z. You never graduate from the cross. You just see more of its beauty the longer you stare at it.

The Long Obedience in the Same Direction

We live in a world of instant gratification. We want 2-minute noodles, 30-second TikToks, and same-day delivery. We are used to things happening fast. But spiritual growth is slow. It is more like growing an oak tree than downloading an app. There will be seasons in your life where you feel "on fire" for God. You will come back from a summer camp or a retreat feeling like you could conquer the world. You will read your Bible for an hour a day and pray with passion.

But then, February comes. The "spiritual high" wears off. You get tired. God feels distant. The Bible feels boring. You might wonder, "Did I lose my faith? Is something wrong with me?"

This is normal. Faith is not a feeling; it is a commitment. Eugene Peterson called the Christian life "a long obedience in the same direction." It is easy to be a Christian when the music is playing and everyone is emotional. It is hard to be a Christian on a Tuesday morning when you failed a test and your friends are being mean. But that is where real faith is forged.

"Keep Going" means you develop **Holy Habits**. You don't brush your teeth only when you feel inspired by dental hygiene; you do it because you want to keep your teeth. In the same way, you don't read the Bible only when you feel "spiritual"; you read it because you need to eat. You don't go to church only when you like the preacher; you go because you need the family. When the feelings fade, the habits hold you.

Think of a train. The engine is **Fact** (the truth of God's Word). The coal car is **Faith** (your trust in the engine). The caboose is **Feeling**. If you try to let the caboose pull the train, you will go nowhere. Feelings follow facts and faith. Don't let your emotions drive the train. Keep shoveling the coal of faith into the engine of truth, even when you don't feel like it. The feelings will eventually catch up.

Facing the inevitable Doubts

As you get older, you will face questions you haven't thought of yet. You might go to college and have a professor who mocks the Bible. You might see a tragedy on the news and wonder, "How can a good God allow this?" You might have a prayer that goes unanswered for years.

When this happens, do not panic. Doubt is not the opposite of faith. Silence is the opposite of faith. Doubt can actually be a growing pain. It is your mind trying to fit a big God into a small box. When the box breaks, it feels scary, but it means you are ready for a bigger view of God.

When you doubt:

1. **Don't doubt alone.** The worst thing you can do is isolate yourself. Talk to a parent, a pastor, or a wise mentor. Tell them, "I'm struggling with X." You will likely find that they have struggled with it too.

2. **Doubt your doubts.** We often question God, but we rarely question our own questions. Why do you feel this way? Is it because of a fact, or because of a disappointment? Are you doubting God because the evidence is bad, or because you want

to live a certain way that God forbids?

3. **Keep eating.** If you are sick and lose your appetite, you still have to eat to get better. If you are spiritually sick with doubt, don't stop reading the Bible or praying. Keep feeding your soul while you look for answers.

The Mission: You Are a Theologian Now

Finally, remember that this theology is not for you to keep in a jar. It is for you to share. You are now a carrier of the cure. The world is sick with sin. People are confused about who they are, why they are here, and where they are going. You have the answers to the test. You know the Creator. You know the Savior. You know the end of the story.

You don't have to be a preacher to share this. You just have to be a witness. A witness in a courtroom doesn't have to argue the case or convince the jury; they just have to tell what they saw and heard. "I was lost, and Jesus found me. I was anxious, and He gave me peace. I was guilty, and He forgave me." That is your testimony.

As you go into high school, college, and your career, you are an ambassador of the Kingdom of Heaven. When you are honest when everyone else cheats, you are doing theology. When you are kind to the person everyone else ignores, you are doing theology. When you forgive someone who hurt you, you are showing them the Cross.

The Final Charge

In the book of Hebrews, the author gives us a picture of a great race. He says we are surrounded by a "great cloud of witnesses", all the believers who have gone before us. Moses, David, Esther, Peter, Paul, your grandmother who prayed for you—they are all in the stands of the stadium, cheering you on.

They are shouting, "Keep going! It's worth it! The struggle is temporary, but the glory is eternal! Don't give up!"

Jesus is at the finish line. He is the "founder and perfecter of our faith." He ran the race first to show us how. He endured the cross for the joy set before Him. Now, it is your turn to run.

Don't run to earn His love; run because you already have it.

Don't run to get saved; run because you are saved.

Don't run alone; run with the Church.

Take the map you have built in these 12 chapters. Put it in your backpack. Tie your shoes. Look at the finish line.

Ready? Set?

Keep Going.

Apply and Act: Your Lifetime Roadmap for Spiritual Growth

This final application section is different. It is not just for this week. It is a set of tools and plans for the rest of your life. This is your survival kit for the long journey ahead.

1. The "Theology in Real Life" Future Forecast

Let's look at how the specific doctrines you learned will help you in future adult situations. Fill in the blanks with how you think that truth will apply.

Future Scenario	Relevant Doctrine	How this Truth Will sustain You
First College Class attacks the Bible	*Bibliology (Inerrancy)*	*I will know that the Bible is historically reliable and God's Word, so I won't be shaken by one professor's opinion.*
You feel lonely in a new city	*Theology Proper (Omnipresence)*	
You mess up big time at a job	*Soteriology (Justification)*	
A loved one gets very sick	*Eschatology (Resurrection)*	

You don't know who to marry/date	*Pneumatology (Guidance)*	

2. The "Spiritual Emergency" Kit

Write down 5 Bible verses that will be your "Emergency Contacts" when things get tough. Memorize these.

1. **For Anxiety:** (e.g., Philippians 4:6-7)

    ----

2. **For Guilt:** (e.g., 1 John 1:9)

    ----

3. **For Loneliness:** (e.g., Psalm 23)

    ----

4. **For Temptation:** (e.g., 1 Corinthians 10:13)

    ----

5. **For Doubt:** (e.g., Mark 9:24)

    ----

3. The "3-Year-Old" Challenge

Albert Einstein said, "If you can't explain it simply, you don't understand it well enough."

- Imagine a 3-year-old asks you: "Who is Jesus?"
- Write a 2-sentence answer using the theology you learned (Christology), but simple enough for a toddler.

    ----

4. Developing Your "Rule of Life" (Expanded)

We touched on this in Chapter 10, but let's make a sustainable plan for the "Long Obedience."

- **The Intake:** I will read the Bible for ____ minutes per day, at this time: __________.

- **The Outpour:** I will serve others/church ____ times per month.
- **The Rest:** I will take a "Sabbath" (rest from work/school) on this day: __________.
- **The Community:** I will meet with other Christians for encouragement (Youth Group/Small Group) on this day: __________.

5. Case Study: The Deconstruction

You have a friend named Taylor. After high school, Taylor stops going to church and posts on Instagram: "I'm deconstructing my faith. The church is full of hypocrites, and I don't think God is real anymore."

- **Empathy:** How do you respond with love instead of judgment?

- **Theology:** How does your knowledge of *Ecclesiology* (the church is made of broken sinners) help you explain why hypocrites exist without disproving God?

- **Action:** What is the best way to "witness" to Taylor in this season? (Hint: Is it an argument or a friendship?)

  ----

6. The "Doxology" Reflection

Read the lyrics to the "Doxology" below. This is a short hymn sung by the church for hundreds of years.

"Praise God from whom all blessings flow; Praise Him all creatures here below; Praise Him above ye heavenly host; Praise Father, Son, and Holy Ghost. Amen."

- **Father:** Why do you praise Him?

- **Son:** Why do you praise Him?

- **Holy Ghost:** Why do you praise Him?

----

7. The "Ebenezers" (Stones of Remembrance)

In the Old Testament, Samuel set up a stone and called it "Ebenezer," saying, "Thus far the Lord has helped us."

- Look back at your life so far. List three specific times God helped you, answered a prayer, or guided you.

    1. ____

    2. ____

    3. ____

- Whenever you doubt God in the future, come back and read this list.

----

8. Recommended Reading List (The Next Steps)

You finished this intro book. Here are three types of books to look for next to keep growing:

- **A Biography:** Read about a missionary or a saint (like *The Hiding Place* by Corrie ten Boom or *Through Gates of Splendor* by Elisabeth Elliot).

- **A Devotional:** Something to help you pray (like *My Utmost for His Highest* or *New Morning Mercies*).

- **A Deeper Theology Book:** (Ask your pastor for a recommendation suited to your age).

9. The Great Commission Contract

Read **Matthew 28:18-20**. This is your job description.

- **"Go":** Where is your current "mission field"? (School, team, neighborhood).

- **"Make Disciples"**: Who is one person you can invite to church or read the Bible with?

- **"I am with you always"**: How does this promise give you the courage to sign your name below?

Signed (Your Name): ____________________

Date: ________________________________

A Final Letter to the Reader

Dear Friend,

If we were sitting across from each other at a coffee shop right now, I would tell you that I am proud of you. Studying God is the hardest and most rewarding work you can do.

But I would also tell you that the best days are ahead of you. Following Jesus is an adventure. It is not safe, He is, as C.S. Lewis wrote, "not a tame lion." He will ask you to do hard things. He will ask you to forgive people who don't deserve it. He will ask you to give your money and your time to help the poor. He will ask you to stand up for the truth when it costs you popularity.

But He will also give you a joy that the world cannot understand. He will give you a peace that makes no sense in the middle of a storm. He will give you a purpose that is bigger than making money or being famous. He will give you Himself.

Don't settle for a shallow faith. Don't settle for a "Sunday-only" religion. Dive into the deep end. Read the hard parts of the Bible. Pray big prayers. Love the unlovable.

You have the map. You have the gear. You have the Guide.

Keep Going.

To help you review, here is a quick "Cheat Sheet" of the big theological words we covered in this book. Keep this handy!

The Word	The Chapter	The Simple Definition
Bibliology	Ch 1	The study of the Bible; how God speaks to us.
Revelation	Ch 1	God showing us who He is (General: Nature; Special: Bible/Jesus).
Inerrancy	Ch 1	The Bible is completely true and without error in what it teaches.
Theology Proper	Ch 2	The study of God the Father and His attributes.
Trinity	Ch 3	God is One in essence, but Three in Person (Father, Son, Spirit).
Anthropology	Ch 4	The study of humanity; we are made in the Image of God (*Imago Dei*).
Hamartiology	Ch 5	The study of sin; "missing the mark."
Christology	Ch 6	The study of Jesus; fully God and fully man.

The Word	The Chapter	The Simple Definition
Incarnation	Ch 6	God becoming flesh (Jesus being born).
Atonement	Ch 6	Jesus paying the penalty for our sin on the cross.
Pneumatology	Ch 7	The study of the Holy Spirit; the Helper.
Soteriology	Ch 8	The study of salvation; how God rescues us.
Justification	Ch 8	God declaring us "righteous" the moment we believe.
Sanctification	Ch 10	The process of becoming more holy over time.
Ecclesiology	Ch 9	The study of the Church; the Body of Christ.
Angelology	Ch 11	The study of angels, demons, and spiritual warfare.
Eschatology	Ch 12	The study of the end times and the return of Jesus.

EXTRA WORKBOOK SECTION
THE DEEP DIVE

You have finished the book. You have read the chapters, learned the big words, and hopefully started to see God in a bigger way. But reading about swimming is not the same as jumping into the ocean. Up until now, we have been wading in the shallow end—getting comfortable with the water, learning the strokes, and understanding the basics. Now, it is time to go deeper.

This **Extra Workbook Section** is designed to be your companion for the next few months. It is not something you rush through in a weekend. It is a toolkit. Think of it like a gym membership for your soul. You don't go to the gym once for 12 hours and expect to be fit; you go for 45 minutes, three times a week, for a year. That is how spiritual growth happens.

This section is divided into five parts:

1. **Bible Study Methods:** Tools to help you feed yourself from God's Word.

2. **Theology in Culture:** How to keep your faith when the world is loud.

3. **Apologetics Bootcamp:** How to defend what you believe.

4. **Prayer & Fasting:** How to connect with God's heart.

5. **Service & Mission:** How to be the hands and feet of Jesus.

Grab a pen, a Bible, and maybe a cup of coffee. Let's get to work.

Part 1: The "Deep Dive" Bible Study Methods

Many teens struggle with reading the Bible because they don't know *how* to read it. They open it up, read a random verse, get confused, and close it. This section will teach you four specific methods to study Scripture. These are tools you can use for the rest of your life.

Method 1: The S.O.A.P. Method

This is the classic, go-to method for daily devotions. It is simple enough to do in 15 minutes but deep enough to change your day.

- **S - Scripture:** Write out the verse or passage you are studying. Writing it helps you slow down and see details you might miss just by reading.
- **O - Observation:** What do you see? Who is talking? What is the context? Are there any repeating words? What is the mood of the passage? (Don't interpret yet; just observe).
- **A - Application:** How does this apply to me *today*? Is there a command to obey? A sin to avoid? A promise to claim? Be specific.
- **P - Prayer:** Write a short prayer back to God based on what you just read.

Guided Exercise: Let's practice with **Psalm 1:1-3**. *"Blessed is the man who walks not in the counsel of the wicked, nor stands in the way of sinners, nor sits in the seat of scoffers; but his delight is in the law of the Lord, and on his law he meditates day and night. He is like a tree planted by streams of water that yields its fruit in its season, and its leaf does not wither. In all that he does, he prospers."*

Your Turn:

- **Scripture:** (Copy the verses above in your own handwriting here):

- **Observation:** (List 3 things you notice. Example: The progression of "walk, stand, sit.")

  1. ____

  2. ____

  3. ____

- **Application:** (How does the "counsel of the wicked" look in your school? Who are you listening to?)

- **Prayer:** (Ask God to help you delight in His law).

Method 2: The Character Study

The Bible is full of flawed people used by a perfect God. Studying their lives helps us see how God interacts with humans. **The Steps:**

1. **Pick a Person:** (e.g., Peter, Ruth, David, Esther).

2. **Gather the References:** Use a concordance or online Bible tool to find where they appear.

3. **Ask the "Big Three" Questions:**
    - What were their strengths?
    - What were their weaknesses/sins?
    - What did they learn about God?

Guided Exercise: The Apostle Peter

- **Passages to Read:** Luke 5:1-11 (The Call), Matthew 14:28-31 (Walking on Water), Matthew 26:69-75 (The Denial), John 21:15-19 (The Restoration).

- **Strengths:** (e.g., Boldness, willingness to step out of the boat).

    ____

    ____

- **Weaknesses:** (e.g., Fear of man, speaking without thinking).

    ____

    ____

- **The Lesson:** How did Jesus treat Peter after he messed up? What does this tell you about how Jesus treats you?

    ____

    ____

Method 3: The Verse Mapping

This is for the visual learners. Verse mapping involves breaking a verse down diagrammatically. You circle key words, draw lines to connect thoughts, and look up definitions of original Greek or Hebrew words.

Guided Exercise: Romans 12:2 *"Do not be conformed to this world, but be transformed by the renewal of your mind, that by testing you may discern what is the will of God, what is good and acceptable and perfect."*

1. **Circle "Conformed":** Look up the definition. (It means "poured into a mold").

    Reflection: What "molds" is the world trying to pour you into right now? (e.g., The mold of popularity, the mold of greed).

    ----

2. **Box "Transformed":** The Greek word is *metamorphoo* (where we get "metamorphosis").

    Reflection: How is a butterfly different from a caterpillar? How should a Christian be different from their old self?

    ----

3. **Underline "Renewal of your mind":**

    Reflection: What are you feeding your mind? (TikTok, Netflix, Scripture?). Garbage in, garbage out.

Method 4: The Keyword Trace

Sometimes a single word can unlock a huge theological truth. **The Word:** *Shalom* (Peace).

1. **Old Testament Meaning:** It doesn't just mean "no war." It means wholeness, completeness, everything working as it should.

2. **New Testament Fulfillment:** Jesus is the "Prince of Peace."

3. **Your Study:** Find 3 verses that use the word "Peace."

    o   Verse 1: ____

    o   Verse 2: ____

    o   Verse 3: ____

    o   **Synthesis:** Based on these verses, is peace a feeling or a fact? ____

We do not live in a bubble. We live in a world that is constantly preaching a sermon to us. Every movie, every song, and every advertisement is telling you what the "good life" is. Theology helps you put on "Jesus Glasses" so you can see the lies and find the truth.

Challenge 1: The Playlist Audit

Music is powerful because it bypasses our logic and goes straight to our emotions. **The Task:** Pick the top 3 songs on your current "On Repeat" playlist. **The Analysis:**

1. **Song Title:**

    ----

2. **The Message:** What is the singer saying will make them happy? (Money, a relationship, **revenge**, partying).

    ----

3. **The Theology Check:** Compare that message to Scripture.
    - *Song says:* "I need you to complete me."
    - *Bible says:* "You are complete in Christ" (Colossians 2:10).
    - *Verdict:* Is this song telling the truth, a lie, or a half-truth?

Challenge 2: The Movie Watch-Along

Next time you watch a movie, don't just consume it; critique it. **The Movie:**

The Questions:

1. **The Villain:** Why is the bad guy bad? usually, it's because they want power, or they are hurt. How does this reflect the biblical idea of sin?

    ----

2. **The Hero:** Does the hero sacrifice themselves? Almost every great movie has a "Christ-figure"—someone who gives up their life for others. Why do you think human beings love that story so much?

----

3. **The Redemption:** How is the problem solved? Is it through violence, forgiveness, or love?

Challenge 3: The Social Media Detox

Social media is designed to make you compare your "behind-the-scenes" with everyone else's "highlight reel." **The Audit:** Go through your "Following" list on Instagram or TikTok.

1. **Identify:** Find 3 accounts that consistently make you feel jealous, angry, or lustful.

   o *Account 1:* ____

   o *Account 2:* ____

   o *Account 3:* ____

2. **The Action:** Mute or Unfollow them for 30 days.

3. **The Replacement:** Find 3 accounts that encourage your faith or teach you something valuable.

   o *Account 1:* ____

   o *Account 2:* ____

   o *Account 3:* ____

Challenge 4: The News Prayer Cycle

Instead of getting anxious about the headlines, turn them into prayer requests. **Current Event:**

- **Who is hurting?** Pray for their comfort.

- **Who is leading?** Pray for wisdom for the politicians/leaders involved.

- **Where is the Church?** Pray for the Christians in that area to be a light.

Part 3: The "Apologetics" Bootcamp

"Apologetics" comes from the Greek word *apologia*, which means "to give a defense." 1 Peter 3:15 says, "Always be prepared to make a defense to anyone who asks you for a reason for the hope that is in you."

You will face questions. Here is how to answer three of the biggest ones.

Unit 1: Does God Exist?

The Argument from Design (Teleological Argument): Imagine you are walking on a beach and find a smartphone in the sand. You pick it up, turn it on, and see it has apps, a camera, and a battery. Would you assume that the sand and the waves just randomly crashed together for millions of years and accidentally formed the phone? No. You would assume a designer made it. The universe is far more complex than a smartphone. The distance of the earth from the sun, the tilt of the axis, the complexity of the human eye, all of these are "fine-tuned" for life.

- **The Defense:** "The universe has a complex design. A design requires a Designer. Therefore, the universe has a Designer."

The Argument from Morality: Every culture in history knows that certain things (like murdering a child for fun) are wrong. Where does this "moral law" come from? If we are just accidents of evolution, "wrong" is just a matter of opinion. But we feel deep down that "wrong" is real.

- **The Defense:** "If there is a Moral Law, there must be a Moral Lawgiver."

Unit 2: Why is there Evil?

This is the hardest question. "If God is all-good and all-powerful, why do bad things happen?" **The Free Will Defense:** God wanted to create a world where love was possible. For love to be real, it must be free. You cannot force a robot to love you. But if you give creatures the freedom to love, you also give them the freedom *not* to love, to hate, to kill, and to sin. Evil is the result of humans misusing their freedom. **The "Soul-Making" Theodicy:** God is more interested in your character than your comfort. Often, we grow the most during hard times. A gym trainer makes you lift heavy weights not because he hates you, but because he wants you to be strong. God can use suffering to make us more like Jesus.

- **The Defense:** "God has not removed evil yet, but He has defeated it at the cross, and one day He will remove it forever."

Unit 3: Is the Bible Reliable?

"Isn't the Bible just a game of telephone? Hasn't it been changed over thousands of years?" **The Manuscript Evidence:** We have more ancient copies of the New Testament than any other book in history.

- *Caesar's Gallic Wars:* written 50 BC, earliest copy 900 AD (Gap: 950 years). Copies: 10.

- *New Testament:* written 50-90 AD, earliest fragments 120 AD (Gap: 30-70 years). Copies: Over 5,800 in Greek alone. **The Archaeological Evidence:** Time and again, archaeology confirms the Bible. We have found the Pool of Siloam, the Pilate Stone, and the walls of Jericho.

- **The Defense:** "The Bible is the best-attested document of ancient history. We can trust that what we have today is what was written then."

Roleplay: The Skeptical Friend Imagine your friend Sam says: *"I believe in science, not fairy tales. Religion is just a crutch for weak people."*

- **How would you respond with gentleness and respect?** (Hint: Ask questions. "What do you mean by 'crutch'?" "Do you think science can answer questions about love or purpose?")

Prayer is the breath of the soul. If you stop breathing, you die. If you stop praying, your faith withers.

Section 1: The A.C.T.S. Model

If you get stuck and don't know what to say, use this acronym.

- **A - Adoration:** Praising God for who He is. "God, You are..."
- **C - Confession:** Admitting where you messed up. "God, I am sorry for..."
- **T - Thanksgiving:** Thanking God for what He has done. "God, thank You for..."
- **S - Supplication:** Asking God for what you need. "God, please help..."

Practice: Write a 4-sentence prayer using ACTS right now.

1. (A) ____
2. (C) ____
3. (T) ____
4. (S) ____

Section 2: Listening Prayer

We often treat prayer like a voicemail where we leave a message and hang up. But it is a conversation. **The Exercise:** Set a timer for 3 minutes. Close your eyes. Do not talk. Just sit in silence and ask, "God, do you want to say anything to me?"

- *Note:* God usually speaks through a quiet thought, a Bible verse popping into your head, or a sense of peace. He will never contradict His Bible.

- **What came to mind during the silence?**

    ____
    ____

Section 3: A Teen's Guide to Fasting

Fasting is voluntarily giving up something good for a spiritual purpose. It tells your body, "I need God more than I need this." **What can you fast from?**

- **Food:** (Skip one meal, like lunch. Note: If you have any history of eating disorders, talk to a doctor or parent first and fast from something else).
- **Technology:** (No Instagram for 24 hours).
- **Entertainment:** (No video games or Netflix for a weekend).

The Purpose: Every time your stomach growls or you reach for your phone, use that as a reminder to pray. **Your Plan:**

- I will fast from:

  ____

- For this long:

  ____

- My spiritual goal is:

  ____

Section 4: The 7-Day Prayer Challenge

Commit to praying for these specific things for the next week.

- **Day 1:** Your Family (Unity, health, salvation).
- **Day 2:** Your School (For bullying to stop, for teachers).
- **Day 3:** Your Pastors/Leaders (For strength, protection from temptation).
- **Day 4:** The Unsaved (List 3 friends who don't know Jesus).
- **Day 5:** The Global Church (Christians being persecuted in other countries).
- **Day 6:** Your Future (Your future spouse, career, calling).
- **Day 7:** Yourself (For purity, wisdom, and courage).

Part 5: The "Service & Mission" Project Planner

Christianity is not a spectator sport. You have a jersey, and you are on the field.

Step 1: Discover Your Gifts

Read the list below and circle the ones that resonate with you.

- **Serving:** You see a mess and clean it up. You like helping behind the scenes.

- **Teaching:** You like explaining things so people understand.
- **Encouragement:** You love cheering people up and writing notes.
- **Giving:** You love being generous with your money or stuff.
- **Leadership:** People naturally follow you when you have an idea.
- **Mercy:** You feel deep sadness for people who are hurting or lonely.
- **Hospitality:** You love making people feel welcome and comfortable.

My Top 2 Gifts seem to be:

1. ____
2. ____

Step 2: Map Your Neighborhood

Who is around you?

- **The Elderly Neighbor:** Does their lawn need mowing? Do they need someone to talk to?
- **The Single Mom:** Could she use a free babysitter for a night?
- **The "Weird" Kid at School:** Do they sit alone at lunch?
- **The Teacher:** Do they look stressed? Could you write them a thank-you note?

One specific need I see right now is:

____

____

Step 3: The "Micro-Mission" Ideas

You don't need to go to Africa to be a missionary. You can start in your kitchen. **Pick one of these to do THIS WEEK:**

- [　] Bake cookies for a neighbor and leave a note saying, "God loves you and so do I."
- [　] Text 3 friends and ask, "How can I pray for you today?"
- [　] Donate your old clothes to a shelter.
- [　] Ask your parents, "What is one chore you hate doing?" and do it for them without being asked.

Step 4: Sharing the Gospel

If someone asked you, "How do I become a Christian?" would you know what to say? Here are two simple methods. Learn one of them.

Method A: The Roman Road Using verses from the book of Romans to explain salvation.

1. **The Problem:** Romans 3:23 ("All have sinned...").

2. **The Consequence:** Romans 6:23 ("The wages of sin is death...").

3. **The Solution:** Romans 5:8 ("But God shows his love for us in that while we were still sinners, Christ died for us").

4. **The Response:** Romans 10:9 ("If you confess... and believe... you will be saved").

Method B: The Three Circles

1. **Circle 1: God's Design.** God made a perfect world full of love.

2. **The Arrow:** Sin took us away from God's design.

3. **Circle 2: Brokenness.** We are now in a broken world (pain, death). We try to fix it with money or popularity (squiggly lines), but they just snap back.

4. **Circle 3: The Gospel.** Jesus came into our brokenness, died, and rose again.

5. **The Response:** If we turn (repent) and believe, we are restored to God's Design.

Practice: Write out the Roman Road verses on an index card and keep it in your wallet/backpack.

EXTRA WORKBOOK SECTION
TEAMWORK

Welcome to the Teamwork Section. If you are reading this, it means you have decided to do something radical. In a world that prizes independence, "self-made" success, and digital isolation, you have chosen to walk the road of faith with others.

Christianity was never designed to be a solo sport. When Jesus started His ministry, the very first thing He did was build a small group. He didn't write a book; He called twelve disciples. He knew that for the truth to survive and for hearts to change, people needed *koinonia*—the Greek word for deep, shared life.

There is a dangerous myth in modern culture called the "Lone Wolf" Christian. This is the person who says, "I love Jesus, but I don't need the church. I can worship God on a hike or in my bedroom just fine." While it is true that you can worship God anywhere, it is impossible to grow into the full image of Christ by yourself. You cannot learn patience without someone to annoy you. You cannot learn forgiveness without someone to hurt you. You cannot learn to serve without someone who has needs.

This workbook section is designed for a group of 3 to 12 friends. You can do this as a youth small group, a lunch club at school, or just a few friends hanging out in a living room. It is a **5-Week Journey** that will take the theology you learned in the main book and force you to live it out in community.

Ground Rules for the Journey:

1. **Commitment:** If you are in, be in. Show up for all 5 weeks.

2. **Confidentiality:** What is said in the room stays in the room. This is the "Vegas Rule" of small groups. If people don't feel safe, they won't be real.

3. **Honesty:** Leave the masks at the door. You don't have to impress anyone here. We are all messy, and we are all in need of grace.

4. **Bible-Centered:** Our opinions are interesting, but God's Word is authoritative. We will always come back to the Text.

How to Use This Section:

- **Designate a Facilitator:** This doesn't have to be a teacher or an adult. It's just someone to read the questions and keep the conversation moving.
- **Bring Supplies:** You will need Bibles, journals, pens, and occasionally some paper or a whiteboard.
- **Pray First:** Never start a session without asking the Holy Spirit to be present.

Week 1: The Foundation (Unmasking)

Objective: To move from shallow friendship to spiritual brotherhood/sisterhood by sharing our stories and establishing a "Covenant of Grace."

Part 1: The Setup (15 Minutes)

Facilitator Read: "We are starting Week 1. The goal today is simple: we want to know who we actually are. Most of us wear masks at school. We have a 'Cool Mask,' a 'Smart Mask,' or a 'Funny Mask.' We wear them to protect ourselves because we are afraid that if people saw our real struggles, they wouldn't like us. But the Gospel says we are fully known by God and still fully loved. That gives us the courage to drop the masks with each other."

Icebreaker: "The Photo Scroll"

- Everyone take out your phone.
- Scroll back to a photo from at least 1 year ago.
- Show the group and explain: *What was happening in this photo? What is one thing you loved about that time, and one thing that was hard about that time that the camera didn't capture?*

Part 2: The Theology of "One Another" (20 Minutes)

Bible Study: Have someone read **Romans 12:3-13** aloud.

Discussion Questions:

1. **Verse 5** says we are "individually members one of another." This is a weird phrase. It suggests we belong to each other, like a hand belongs to an arm.

- ○ *Question:* Do you usually feel like you "belong" to the other Christians in your life? Why or why not?

2. **Verse 9** says, "Let love be genuine." The Greek word here is *anypokritos*, which means "without a mask" or "not acting."
   - ○ *Question:* What does "fake love" look like in a friend group? What does "genuine love" look like?
3. **Verse 10** says, "Outdo one another in showing honor."
   - ○ *Question:* Imagine a competition where everyone is trying to honor the other person more. How would that change the vibe of your school or group?

Part 3: The Activity - "Life Maps" (45 Minutes)

Materials Needed: Large sheets of paper and markers for everyone.

Instructions: You are going to draw a "Map" of your life journey so far. This isn't an art contest; it's a way to visualize your story.

1. **The Start:** Draw a symbol for where you were born or your early family life.
2. **The Highs:** Draw "Mountains" for the best moments (e.g., winning a championship, a great vacation, getting saved).
3. **The Lows:** Draw "Valleys" for the hardest moments (e.g., parents divorcing, moving schools, a health struggle, a season of depression).
4. **The Turns:** Draw "Road Signs" for moments where your life changed direction (e.g., meeting a certain friend, a youth camp, a bad choice).
5. **The Current Location:** Draw a symbol for where you are right now with God (e.g., a desert, a garden, a battlefield, a fog).

Sharing: Give everyone 10-15 minutes to draw. Then, go around the circle. Each person has 3-5 minutes to explain their map.

- *Crucial Rule:* While someone is sharing, no one interrupts. You just listen. At the end, simply say, "Thank you for sharing," or "I appreciate your honesty."

Reflection:

- Did you learn something new about someone you thought you knew well?
- Did you see any common themes in the "Valleys" of the group?

Part 4: The Covenant (10 Minutes)

Facilitator Read: "Now that we have shared our stories, we need to agree on how we will treat each other. A 'Covenant' is a serious promise. It is heavier than a contract."

The Group Covenant: Read these aloud together. If everyone agrees, sign a piece of paper with these points written on it.

- **I Promise Confidentiality:** I will not gossip about what is shared here.
- **I Promise Grace:** I will not judge you for your struggles, but point you to Jesus.
- **I Promise Truth:** I will speak the truth in love, even when it is hard.
- **I Promise Prayer:** I will pray for this group during the week.

Part 5: Closing Prayer (5 Minutes)

Don't just have one person pray. Do "Popcorn Prayer."

- Everyone pick one person on their right.
- Pray one sentence for that person based on the "Life Map" they shared.
- (Example: "Lord, please help Sarah in the 'valley' she is in right now.")

Homework for Week 2: Read **Colossians 3:1-17** every day this week. Just read it. Don't study it yet. Just let it soak in.

Week 2: The Study (Digging Deeps)

Objective: To learn how to feed ourselves from the Bible *together* using the Inductive Bible Study Method, moving from passive listening to active discovery.

Part 1: The Warm-Up (10 Minutes)

Check-In:

- How was your week?
- Did anyone actually read Colossians 3? Be honest!
- *Theology Recap:* Who remembers what **Sanctification** means? (Answer: The process of becoming holy/more like Jesus). Today, we are going to look at the "Instruction Manual" for Sanctification.

Part 2: The Method - Observation (20 Minutes)

Facilitator Note: "We are going to be detectives today. We are looking at **Colossians 3:1-17**. We will use three steps: Observation (What does it say?), Interpretation (What does it mean?), and Application (What do I do?)."

Read Colossians 3:1-17 Aloud. (Ideally, have different people read 3 verses each).

Group Exercise: The Whiteboard Deconstruction (If you don't have a whiteboard, use a big piece of paper in the middle of the room).

Ask the group to shout out "Observations." Write them down.

- *Look for Contrasts:* What is being compared? (e.g., "Things above" vs. "Things on earth").
- *Look for Commands:* What are we told to do? (e.g., "Seek," "Set your minds," "Put to death").
- *Look for Lists:* There are two lists in this passage—a "Kill List" (verses 5-9) and a "Wear List" (verses 12-14). Let's list them out side-by-side.

The Lists (Write these out):

- **Put to Death (The Old Self):** Evil desire, covetousness, anger, wrath, malice, slander, obscene talk, lying.
- **Put On (The New Self):** Compassionate hearts, kindness, humility, meekness, patience, bearing with one another, forgiveness, love, peace, thankfulness.

Part 3: The Deep Dive - Interpretation (30 Minutes)

Discussion Questions:

1. **The "Clothing" Metaphor:** Paul uses the language of changing clothes ("put off" and "put on").
   - *Question:* Why is this a good picture of the Christian life? Can you wear "clean clothes" (kindness) over "dirty clothes" (anger)? No, you have to take the old off first.
   - *Theology Check:* This relates to **Justification** vs. **Sanctification**. We *are* new creations (Justification), but we have to *choose* to dress like it (Sanctification).

2. **The "Kill" List:** Look at verse 5. It says "Put to death." It doesn't say "manage" or "suppress."

   - *Question:* Why does the Bible use such violent language for sin? What happens if you try to "tame" a sin like greed or lust instead of killing it?
   - *Discussion:* Which of the sins in the "Put to Death" list do you think is most accepted in high school culture today? (e.g., Slander/Gossip is often seen as normal).

3. **The "Super-Glue" of Love:** Verse 14 says, "And above all these put on love, which binds everything together in perfect harmony."

   - *Question:* Imagine you have patience and humility but no love. What does that look like? (Maybe you are just acting polite but secretly resentful). Why is love the "binder"?

Part 4: The Application Grid (20 Minutes)

Activity: Give everyone a piece of paper. Draw a grid with 4 squares. Label them:

1. **Home/Family**
2. **School/Work**
3. **Friends/Group**
4. **Enemies/Annoying People**

Instructions: Pick **ONE** quality from the "Put On" list (Compassion, Kindness, Humility, Meekness, Patience, Forgiveness). Write that quality in the middle of the page. Now, write one specific action you can do in each square to show that quality this week.

- *Example: Patience.*
  - *Home:* I will not snap at my mom when she asks about homework.
  - *School:* I will wait for the slow walker in the hallway without sighing.
  - *Friends:* I will listen to [Name]'s story without interrupting.
  - *Enemies:* I will pray for the person who bullied me instead of roasting them.

Share: Ask for volunteers to share one of their application points.

Part 5: Worship & Word (10 Minutes)

Verse 16 says, "Let the word of Christ dwell in you richly... singing psalms and hymns and spiritual songs."

- If your group is musical, sing a song together (acapella or with a guitar).
- If not, play a worship song on a speaker.
- *Challenge:* Don't just listen. Sing. Make it a declaration that you are "Putting On" the new self.

Homework for Week 3: Identify one "Stronghold" or persistent struggle in your life (e.g., anxiety, lust, anger, procrastination). Come ready to talk about it next week (as much as you feel safe).

Week 3: The Battle (Accountability)

Objective: To recognize the reality of spiritual warfare and to set up a system of accountability where we fight *for* each other, not just *with* each other.

Part 1: The War Room Context (10 Minutes)

Facilitator Read: "Welcome to the Bunker. Last week we looked at the clothes we need to wear. Today we look at the armor. We learned in the **Angelology** chapter that we have an enemy. Satan loves to isolate Christians. He knows that a zebra separated from the herd is easy prey. He wants you to keep your struggles secret. He whispers, 'If they knew the truth about you, they would reject you.' Today, we prove him wrong."

Theology Check: Hamartiology (Sin) & **Spiritual Warfare**.

- Sin thrives in the dark.
- Confession brings it into the light.
- James 5:16 says, "Confess your sins to one another and pray for one another, *that you may be healed*." Note: We confess to God for *forgiveness*, but we confess to each other for *healing*.

Part 2: The "Hot Seat" of Grace (40 Minutes)

Disclaimer: This activity requires maturity. The goal is encouragement, not interrogation.

The Concept: We are going to go around the circle. One person is in the "Hot Seat." They will answer two questions:

1. **Where are you winning right now?** (Where do you see God working? What are you proud of?)

2. **Where are you fighting right now?** (What is the struggle you identified for homework? Where are you weak?)

The Rules for the Listeners:

- **No Fixing:** Do not say, "Oh, have you tried this app?" or "You should just read more." Just listen.

- **No Shaming:** Do not gasp or look shocked.

- **Affirmation:** After they share, the group must speak truth over them. (e.g., "I see God's grace in you," or "You are brave for sharing that.")

The Practice: Spend about 5-7 minutes per person. If the group is large (over 8), split into two smaller groups for this.

- *Example Share:* "I am winning in my prayer life; I've prayed every morning. But I am fighting with lust. I keep looking at things I shouldn't on my phone late at night."

- *Example Response:* "Thank you for trusting us. We are with you. You are not defined by that struggle. You are a child of God."

Part 3: The Shield Wall (20 Minutes)

Activity: In ancient Rome, soldiers used a formation called the *testudo* (tortoise). They would lock their shields together. If one soldier dropped his shield, the guy next to him would get hit. We need to lock shields.

Partner Up: Break into pairs (same gender is usually best for this). This is your **"Shield Partner"** for the rest of the month. Exchange phone numbers if you don't have them.

The Assignment: You must text your Shield Partner at least **three times** this week.

- **Text 1 (Check-in):** "How is the battle today?"

- **Text 2 (Scripture):** Send a verse that encourages them.

- **Text 3 (Prayer):** "How can I pray for you right now?"

Discuss in Pairs:

- What is the best time of day to check in?
- What is your "Code Red"? (e.g., If I am really tempted, can I text you "Code Red" and you just pray immediately?)

Part 4: Prayer focus - The Armor (15 Minutes)

Corporate Prayer: Come back together as a big group. We are going to pray through **Ephesians 6:10-18** for the person on our left.

- *Leader:* "Lord, we equip [Name] with the Belt of Truth."
- *Group:* "Let them know what is real and reject the lies."
- *Leader:* "We equip [Name] with the Breastplate of Righteousness."
- *Group:* "Guard their heart and emotions."
- *Leader:* "We equip [Name] with the Shoes of Peace."
- *Group:* "Let them bring peace to their school."
- *Leader:* "We equip [Name] with the Shield of Faith."
- *Group:* "Extinguish every flaming arrow of doubt."
- *Leader:* "We equip [Name] with the Helmet of Salvation."
- *Group:* "Protect their mind and thoughts."
- *Leader:* "We give [Name] the Sword of the Spirit."
- *Group:* "Let Your Word be in their mouth."

Part 5: Conclusion (5 Minutes)

Facilitator Read: "You are no longer fighting alone. When you are tempted this week, remember: there is a Shield Partner and a whole room of people standing with you. Don't drop your shield."

Homework for Week 4: Think of **three people** in your life who do not know Jesus. Write their names down on a card and bring it next week.

Week 4: The Outward Look (The Search Party)

Objective: To turn our focus outward, equipping the team for evangelism and service. We move from the "Bunker" to the "Field."

Part 1: The Huddle (10 Minutes)

Theology Check: Soteriology (Salvation) & **Missiology** (Mission).

- **Soteriology** teaches us that salvation is a free gift of grace.

- **Missiology** teaches us that we are the delivery drivers of that gift.
- **Analogy:** Imagine you found the cure for cancer, but you kept it in your basement while your neighbors were dying. That would be criminal. We have the cure for death (the Gospel). We must share it.

Reflect:

- Why is sharing our faith so scary? (Fear of rejection, not knowing answers, looking weird).
- How does doing it as a *team* make it easier?

Part 2: The Apologetics Dojo (30 Minutes)

Facilitator Note: "We are going to spar. We need to practice answering hard questions so we don't freeze up when they happen in real life."

Roleplay Activity: Split into groups of 3.

- **Person A:** The Skeptic (Ask a tough question).
- **Person B:** The Christian (Answer with gentleness and respect).
- **Person C:** The Coach (Watch and give feedback).

Scenario 1: The "Good Person" Argument

- *Skeptic:* "I don't need Jesus. I'm a good person. I don't kill anyone. If God is real, He'll let me into heaven because I'm nice."
- *Christian Goal:* Explain that God's standard is perfection, not just "niceness," and that's why we need a Savior (Romans 3:23).
- *Coach:* Did they get defensive? Did they use the Bible?

Scenario 2: The "Intolerant" Argument

- *Skeptic:* "Christians are so judgmental. You think you're the only ones who are right. That's arrogant."
- *Christian Goal:* Explain that truth isn't about arrogance; it's about reality. (e.g., "If a doctor tells you have an illness, is he arrogant, or is he trying to help you?"). Focus on Jesus saying "I am the Way" (John 14:6).

Scenario 3: The "Suffering" Argument

- *Skeptic:* "If God loves us, why did my grandma die of cancer?"
- *Christian Goal:* Don't try to solve the mystery of evil. Show empathy. "I am so sorry about your grandma. The Bible actually says death is an enemy. Jesus hates death too—He wept at a tomb. He came to defeat it."

Switch Roles: Rotate so everyone gets a turn being the Christian.

Part 3: The "Three Circles" Drill (20 Minutes)

Review: Refer back to the "Three Circles" method from the Extra Workbook Section (Brokenness -> God's Design -> Gospel).

Practice: Get a partner. Take 2 minutes each to explain the Gospel to each other using the Three Circles. Use a piece of paper and draw it while you talk.

- *Tip:* Keep it simple. Don't use big "Christianese" words like *Propitiation* or *Sanctification* when talking to a non-believer. Use words like *Broken, Restored, Trust.*

Part 4: The Neighborhood Watch (20 Minutes)

The Name Cards: Take out the cards with the 3 names you wrote down for homework. Place them all in the center of the room (or on a table).

The Prayer Circle: Gather around the names. We are going to pray for them "Harvest Style."

- Pray that God would soften their hearts (The Soil).
- Pray for an opportunity to speak to them this week (The Open Door).
- Pray for courage to invite them to church/youth group (The Invitation).

The Service Project Brainstorm: As a team, you need to do one outward act together this month.

- *Brainstorm ideas:*
    - Buy 20 burgers and hand them out to homeless people downtown.
    - Go to a local park and pick up trash for an hour.

- o Write "Thank You" cards for the school janitors and cafeteria staff and deliver them with donuts.
  - o Offer to do yard work for an elderly neighbor of one of the group members.

Decision: Vote on one project. Set a date. Assign roles (Who buys supplies? Who drives? Who brings the speaker for music?).

Part 5: Closing (10 Minutes)

Facilitator Read: "We are a search party. This week, keep your eyes open. Look for the people on your cards. Look for the lonely. If you see an opportunity, take it. And text your Shield Partner if you get nervous!"

Homework for Week 5: Bring an object that represents your hope for the future (it can be anything—a picture, a tool, a souvenir). Also, write a short letter to *each* person in the group (just 1-2 sentences of encouragement).

Week 5: The Future (The Launchpad)

Objective: To solidify the bonds formed, celebrate growth, and commission the group to live with an eternal perspective.

Part 1: The Theology of Hope (15 Minutes)

Theology Check: Eschatology (The End Times/Future).

- Eschatology isn't just about the end of the world; it's about the goal of history.
- We are moving toward a Wedding Feast (Revelation 19).
- We are moving toward a New Earth where righteousness dwells.
- Because we know the end of the story, we can endure the messy middle chapters.

Discussion:

- Show the "Object of Hope" you brought. Explain why you picked it.
- *Question*: How does knowing that Jesus wins in the end help you when you have a bad day at school?

Part 2: The "Speak Life" Ceremony (40 Minutes)

The Concept: Proverbs 18:21 says, "Death and life are in the power of the tongue." We usually hear a lot of death (criticism, sarcasm, insults). Today, we speak life.

The Activity: One person sits in the middle (or focus on one person at a time in the circle). Everyone else reads the short note/letter they wrote for that person.

- *Specific Encouragement:* Don't just say "You're nice." Say, "I see the gift of leadership in you," or "Your joy makes our group better," or "I admire how you stood up for your faith."
- *Prophetic Encouragement:* "I believe God is going to use you to..."

The Recipient: The person receiving the encouragement cannot deflect it. They cannot say, "Oh, no, I'm not that great." They must simply say, "Thank you, I receive that."

Repeat: Go around until everyone has been encouraged. This will take time, and it will likely be emotional. Let it be. This is *koinonia*.

Part 3: The Covenant Meal (Communion) (20 Minutes)

Facilitator Note: *Check with your church leadership/parents about leading Communion. If you are not comfortable or authorized to do formal Communion, call this a "Covenant Meal" and share food together with spiritual intent.*

The Setup: Have bread/crackers and juice/grapes ready.

The Reading: Read **1 Corinthians 11:23-26**.

The Reflection: Before eating, take a moment of silence.

- Look back at the last 5 weeks.
- Thank Jesus that *He* is the one who made this community possible. His body was broken so we could be the "Body of Christ." His blood was shed to sign the New Covenant.

The Partaking: Serve one another. Pass the bread and juice around.

- As you pass it, say: "The Body of Christ, broken for you." / "The Blood of Christ, shed for you."

The Feast: After the solemn moment, eat! If you brought snacks or a meal (pizza, etc.), transition into hanging out and eating together. The early church always connected Communion with a "Love Feast" (a full meal).

Part 4: The "Time Capsule" (10 Minutes)

Activity: Take a piece of paper. Write a letter to your "Future Self" (Open in 1 Year).

- What did you learn in this study?

- What do you want to remember about God?

- What are you praying for your future self to be doing?

- Who are you praying for?

Seal it: Put it in an envelope. Write the date "Open [Date] Next Year." Give all the envelopes to the Facilitator (or a responsible person) to keep safe, or have everyone keep their own in their Bible.

Part 5: The Final Commissioning (5 Minutes)

Facilitator Read: "We are done with the workbook, but we are not done with the work. The huddle breaks, and the play begins.

- Keep your Covenants.

- Keep texting your Shield Partners.

- Keep looking for the lost.

- Keep your eyes on the King."

The Huddle Break: Everyone stand up. Put hands in the middle. Facilitator prays a loud prayer of sending. **"1, 2, 3... GO!"**

Appendix: Resources for the Leader

How to Handle "Awkward Silence"

When you ask a question and no one answers, **wait.** Count to 10 in your head. People are thinking. If the silence goes too long, rephrase the question. "Let me ask it a different way..." Don't answer your own question.

How to Handle the "Over-Talker"

If one person dominates the conversation:

- Affirm them: "Thanks, [Name], that's a great point."

- Pivot: "I'd love to hear from someone who hasn't shared yet. Sarah? Mike?"

- Talk privately: If it continues, pull them aside gently after the meeting. "Hey, I love your passion, but I want to make sure we leave space for the quiet ones to share."

How to Handle "Heavy" Confessions

If someone confesses something serious (self-harm, abuse, suicidal thoughts, serious addiction):

1. **Stay Calm.** Don't freak out.

2. **Thank them.** "Thank you for being brave enough to share that."

3. **Do not keep it a secret.** If it involves safety (abuse or suicide), you *must* tell a trusted adult (Youth Pastor, Parent, Counselor). Remind them of the "Limits of Confidentiality" (we keep secrets unless you are hurting yourself or others are hurting you).

4. **Pray immediately.**

Spotify Playlist Recommendations for Week 2 & 5

- *Elevation Worship* - "Available"
- *Hillsong United* - "Good Grace"
- *Phil Wickham* - "Battle Belongs"
- *Maverick City Music* - "Jireh"
- *Citizens* - "In Tenderness"

Snack Ideas

- *Week 1*: Popcorn (easy, sharable).
- *Week 2*: Sour Patch Kids (sweet and sour, like the "Put Off/Put On" list).
- *Week 3*: Warheads or something intense (for the "Battle").
- *Week 4*: Donuts (round, like the "3 Circles").
- *Week 5*: Pizza party or a Potluck.